Twentieth Century Anthology of American Literature

Edited by

Rupali Saran Mirza

ATLANTIC

PUBLISHERS & DISTRIBUTORS (P) LTD

Published by
ATLANTIC
PUBLISHERS & DISTRIBUTORS (P) LTD
7/22, Ansari Road, Darya Ganj, New Delhi-110002
Phones : +91-11-40775252, 23273880, 23275880, 23280451
Fax : +91-11-23285873
Web : www.atlanticbooks.com
E-mail : orders@atlanticbooks.com

Branch Office
5, Nallathambi Street, Wallajah Road, Chennai-600002
Phones : +91-44-64611085, 32413319
E-mail : chennai@atlanticbooks.com

Reprint 2018

Printed in India at Nice Printing Press, A-33/3A, Site-IV,
Industrial Area, Sahibabad, Ghaziabad, U.P.

Dedicated to

My parents,
Mr. Anant Saran and Mrs. Rekha Saran
and
My family,
Mr. M.A. Abbas (my husband) and
Sarah Fatima Mirza (my daughter)

Foreword

Literature is a continuum. That is why it has a living *Élan vital* and hence is a living testament of human experiences. So are literary criticism and academic studies. Literature grows, matures, changes and modifies itself through a process of convention and revolt. Critical and academic trends also come and go, but do return and revisit *a la mode*. The rise and fall of trends, genres and sub-species of literature are thus what one witnesses in literary histories. Critical and academic trends also do the same. Once upon a time British literature was the in-thing for English studies in the Indian subcontinent. Then the rise of American literature charmed the scholars like a kite flying in the sky and the academic focus tilted towards American literature which ruled the critical thinking for decades. It was around 1970s that we again witnessed the shift of academic focus from English literature, which also included American literature, to literatures in English. Post-colonial literatures designated earlier as Commonwealth literature and New Literatures in English ruled English studies in the Indian subcontinent for almost 45 years. Meanwhile, as is natural, one always searches for roots. And to say it openly, the roots of English studies in the Indian subcontinent lay in British literature and American literature despite the politics of inclusion and exclusion. In the 21st century, young scholars who are now openly responsive to new and varied areas are being once again fascinated with British and American literatures after a spell of flirtation with Post-colonial literatures because one never forgets one's first love. It is, I think, in this perspective that we are, at the moment, having a revival of critical and academic interest in American literature and British literature.

The present collection of critical essays, entitled *Twentieth Century Anthology of American Literature* aims at providing a comprehensive analysis of the twentieth century American literary writings for the academic circles. The essays collected here explore the undercurrents of American literary practices in the select texts written during a definite time period. The current trends lay emphasis on forming new ideas and on critical analysis of the existing texts, which is a change in the intellectual literary tradition that has given rise to critical anthologies. This anthology provides an unbiased and comprehensive account of American literary works of the 20th century by considering the viewpoints of researchers from different countries such as India, Saudi Arabia, Pakistan and Africa. It contains a good coverage and selection of research ideas from academicians and researchers who have expertise in this domain of knowledge.

The select literary works have been analyzed in the perspectives of textual analysis and implied critical literary theory of canonical literary authors such as T.S. Eliot, John Dos Passos, Arthur Miller, Toni Morrison, Lorraine Hansberry, Robert Frost, Neil Simon, Bernard Malamud, Langston Hughes, Norman Mailer, Ayn Rand and Thom Gunn who form the epicentre of discussion. A comprehensive study of the various literary genres, inclusive of prose, poetry and drama, reveals the complex interplay of ideas which ultimately go into the making of different ideologies related to literature in the twentieth century. The pantheon of the chosen literary texts does not undermine the interests of any marginalized section of American literary writings. It is inclusive and representative of women writers, Afro-American writers as well as diasporic communities.

This anthology, I modestly hope, will provide a wide reading to students and teachers in the area of American literature and will prove to be a ready reference resource for researchers. When there is a boom of critical anthologies on Post-colonial literatures, the editor of the present anthology must be congratulated for her daring deviation in the arena of anthology-making.

Dr. S.Z.H. Abidi
Senior Professor, Head and Dean
Department of English, Integral University, Lucknow
Former Professor and Head
Department of English and Modern European Languages
Lucknow University

Preface

Twentieth Century Anthology of American Literature includes outstanding research papers which are different in style and content. An analysis has been attempted of the select and representative works of American writers from the angle of examining the varied nuances of American literature and culture in the twentieth century. This anthology was motivated by the desire to explore American Literature and associated traditions from various perspectives. As my research is also based on investigating the twentieth century American literary masterpieces, this anthology opened doors to undertake a study of other related literary works.

The book will be instrumental in helping the scholars in understanding a plethora of literary writings which have been analyzed critically. It is hoped that this anthology would appeal to the broad scholarship of American Literature as it explains the underlying objectives of American life and psychology. It should also provide the necessary stimulus for researchers to enhance their perception in this domain.

Rupali Saran Mirza

Contents

Introduction

Twentieth century American literature is representative of a period full of important historical events such as the Wall Street Crash, First World War, Second World War and Cold War which culminated in several literary movements, like Romanticism, Realism and Naturalism. The Realists believe in the philosophy that an individual's choice is dependent on external forces. On the other hand, Naturalists following the doctrine of Emile Zola believe that individuals have no choice at all since their life is dependent on their external circumstances as well as their birth. The trend in literary writings was changing to include the experience of the common man. The Industrial Revolution happened between the 18th and 19th centuries, as a result of which there was a spurt of immigration from rural areas to cities. This was the most conducive background for literary Realism which prevailed after Industrialization, when the cities were developing and the agrarian economy was replaced by an industrial economy which was more dependent on machinery and equipment instead of human labour.

Literary Naturalism was a movement which started in the late nineteenth century and continued till early twentieth century. Theodore Dreiser's *Sister Carrie* (1900) came as a pathbreaker which called for acceptance of a naturalistic piece of art. This was the time when the common people were tired of ostentatious manifestations of Romantic Literature. There was an emerging middle class society which wanted a social change. There was also a huge transition from a society enfeebled with slavery to a society which was empowered by the force of democracy. People were becoming more literate and they realized that their real state was represented more appropriately through Naturalism rather than Romanticism.

The transcendentalists like Emerson and Thoreau were followed by the Romantics in early 1800s. These movements were overshadowed by Realism which was a sharp reaction to Romanticism. Romanticism idealized things such as nature and spirituality but Realism de-emphasized plots and paid more attention to reality because real life has no plot, it has only events. Naturalism was a movement which was a further manifestation of Realism. Naturalism too depicts reality of life with the minute difference that the characters portrayed in naturalistic works are overpowered by external circumstances. Thus, one can easily deduce that Naturalism is an extension of Realism. It is a product of chance or fate, environment and heredity, which exercise a huge control over the life of the chief characters in the literary work, who are victims of these external conditions.

Some common themes of Naturalism are objective presentation of the subject just like in a scientific experiment in which the final product takes its form due to the reaction of chemicals because of external surroundings and reactions. There is a rejection of supernatural logic for events like it was done in Romantic Literature. The characters are not dehumanized; therefore, they abide by the laws of nature. Characters are viewed as a product of their environment as also the product of their heredity. Chance and destiny lead to lack of free will; thereby, they fall as unwilling victims of Sociology and Darwinism, and only the fittest survives. Since the naturalists study man as more close to nature, there is less or no filtering of the facts. Thus, we see topics discussed freely, which are otherwise considered as social taboos.

The society of the 1920s, better known as the Jazz Age, was significant for its commodity culture. The upsurge of the Jazz Age continued up to 1929. It signified hedonism. After the First World War (July 1914-November 1918) America was full of triumph and confidence. The young generation was free from the shackles of Puritanism breathing a sigh of relief from the traditional norms that had manacled the society till now. The young generation breaking free from the conventional restraints had declared its new motto of eating, drinking and being merry. Pleasure was the main principle in people's life, which was far from moral. The new society of Jazz Age gave ample freedom to the intermingling of opposite sexes. This revolution of the younger generation was not a passing phase, it culminated into a revolt by people of all ages, especially the middle aged people who adopted the new culture losing their sense of morality and tradition.

The atmosphere was characterized by explicit magazines and movies. There was an increase in the population of bootleggers with the implementation of the Prohibition Act which resulted in an open culture promoting alcoholism. Men would casually carry gin in their pockets. Serving of alcoholic drinks before dinner became a social obligation. The Jazz Age was driven by the Prohibition Act, automobiles, explicit magazines and movies.

The philosophy of the American Dream still continued to be a motivating factor for upward mobility, even after the First World War because the 1900s made the Americans financially more stable. The people were under the notion that happiness, prosperity and success could be achieved through hard work. Europe had incurred huge losses during wartime and was in a dilapidated condition after four years of warfare. America had emerged as one of world's leading powers after the Treaty of Versailles (28 June 1919) . There was an atmosphere of happiness and victory throughout America.

The young generation was now free from the shackles of Puritanism. This generation almost came out with a rebellion and revolted against the puritan orthodox culture. They now wanted new rules which had no cultural underpinnings. They were of the opinion that the older generation had ruined them by establishing an authoritarian code of conduct.

F. Scott Fitzgerald could think of no better than branding this era with an exclusive name, "the Jazz Age". This post-World War age was aptly described so because this was the time which witnessed the upsurge of the youth who did not want to think about their past, nor they thought about their future. They wanted to make the optimum use of their present day. People were financially self-sufficient. Moreover, there was no binding on them to follow traditions; therefore, they wanted to break free just to eat, drink and be merry.

Twentieth century American society followed Bohemian culture. It was more influenced by the teachings of Freud than Jefferson's ideals. People believed in a free spirit, far from their old orthodox values and conservative roots of puritan culture. Fitzgerald's explanation about the term 'Jazz' was: "first sex, then dancing, then music".

The woman of 20th century America was busy chasing her material dreams. The new trend promoted mixed parties in which men and women freely intermingled without any moral police guarding them. The women adopted a lifestyle which made them free individuals. They wore all types of clothes which revealed most of their skin. The boys preferred to wear Jerseys which were without sleeves, just like the dress code of the hero of F. Scott Fitzgerald's *This Side of Paradise* (1920). These shirts were called 'petting shirts.' People were lost in the spirit of Jazz and they found pleasure only in sensuous music and dances. The American woman got the right to vote in the 1920s. This gave her a status equivalent to men. Till then a woman's job was to look after the house but with greater political freedom, there was more economic independence, which widened her circumference and restricted her no more to just household chores. Now women were interested in looking beautiful and stylish and they served as casual and lively counterparts to their male companions.

In the post-First World War decade, Freud and his theories were appreciated by the people. American literature was full of new terminology such as "Electra" and "Oedipus Complex", "Sadism", etc. There was change in every arena of life—fast racing cars, racy magazines, movies—altogether a revolution was in the offing. Men and women not only sang and danced together but also indulged in drinking bouts together. It became common courtesy to serve alcohol before dinner. There was no restriction on consumption of alcohol even among the younger boys.

With access to automobiles, there was nobody stopping the younger generation. It increased their mobility which led to more freedom in making individual choices and decisions. The racing automobiles were soon followed by racy and sensual movies and magazines which had a scintillating effect on American senses. In short, the Doctrine of Freud, more female freedom, the Prohibition Act, movies, magazines and automobiles—all had an effect on the American population in the 1900s. Later, this effect became permanent as the middle aged people now adopted the ways of the younger generation. The Americans were lost in their dream of money and success which they had built upon the ruins of their devastated society after the World War.

The age was symbolic of wealth which was deeply associated with the American Dream. Thus, the age of the "Lost Generation" earmarks the rise of modern American mass culture. All this was an immediate response to the breakdown of the society after World War 1. The Great Depression and World War 1 were the main historical reasons for this moral and cultural breakdown. The term "Lost Generation" was coined by Gertrude Stein to amalgamate all the literary writers who took recluse in Paris after being completely disillusioned by the bloodshed in the First World War (1914-1918). This generation of writers included Faulkner, Hemingway, Fitzgerald and the likes of them. However, the pantheon of 20th century literary writers is much wider than can fit in the aforesaid description.

T.S. Eliot's *The Waste Land* (1922) is a representation of the mass culture that prevailed at that time. A similar portrait can be seen in "The Valley of Ashes", a place vividly pictured in *The Great Gatsby* (1925) by F. Scott Fitzgerald. Both these works can be studied in the light of the major themes that the writers of the Lost Generation wanted to highlight. Alienation and violence is a common theme after the World War and post-Depression period. Society was in a state of decay and most of the protagonists in the literary works which came during these years have a longing for a return to innocence. They also procrastinate most of the times but are unable to take any firm decisions, and therefore, they lack the ability to act. In such an environment, man tries to create his own ideals which are myths, so that he can steer his life clear of the prevailing confusion.

These false ideals and myths led to the rise of philosophers such as Karl Marx, Darwin, Sigmund Freud and C.F. Nietzsche. Freud tried to study the behaviour of man according to psychoanalysis. He felt that man's behaviour was what he thought from inside, it was based on his psychology. Whereas it was external preferences and not internal ones that influenced him. According to Karl Marx, thoughts depict man's behaviour more as a result of outside forces such as economic conditions and class struggle. The agony of the past is reflected in the philosophical doctrine of Nietzsche who declares the "Death of God", which came as an aftermath of World War.

Gertrude Stein said to Ernest Hemingway, "You are all a lost generation" in the epigraph to *The Sun Also Rises* (1926). The term was made popular by the novelist, Ernest Hemingway as he wrote the novel *A Moveable Feast* (1964) which speaks of the Bohemian community in Paris who failed to ascribe to the moral code set by the Victorian writers before them. The Wall Street Crash, better known as the Great Depression, brought a sudden slump in the market economy of America. People lost their jobs, industries were shut down which left the people high and dry. These conditions are vividly portrayed in *The Grapes of Wrath* (1939) by John Steinbeck. Similar was the predicament of Willy Loman, the protagonist of Arthur Miller's *Death of a Salesman* (1949), who had no option but suicide in the post-Depression years when all business was in a slump. In 1940s Miller had realized that the Great Depression had changed the situation for the working class as well as for the deprived sections of the society. The only consequence of the Depression was that it strengthened the stronghold of the factory and firm owners and shattered the hopes of the society which had been generated during the early years of Industrial Revolution. The end of the play, culminating in the suicide of Willy Loman, completely reflects upon the concept of "the American dream" in a new light. It is the story of the collapse of immense belief in an institution under pressure from the demands of the modern way of life. It depicts the pressures which weigh heavy upon the heart and mind of the protagonist who succumbs under them.

1914-1945, and thereafter was the era of Modernism and the era of Experimentation. It was characterized by materialism and ambition for success promised by the American Dream. This journey towards the attainable yet unattainable is full of practical challenges. Ezra Pound (1885-1972), T.S. Eliot (1888-

1965), Robert Frost (1874-1963), Wallace Stevens (1879-1955), William Carlos Williams (1883-1963), Marianne Moore (1887-1972), Robinson Jeffers (1887-1962), Edward Estlin Cummings (1894-1962), Hart Crane (1899-1932), Langston Hughes (1902-1967) were the renowned poets between 1914-1945. Prose was dominated by F. Scott Fitzgerald (1896-1940), Ernest Hemingway (1899-1961), William Faulkner (1897-1962), Sinclair Lewis (1885-1951), John Steinbeck (1902-1968), John Dos Passos (1896-1970) and Richard Wright (1908-1960). Twentieth century American drama was incomplete without Eugene O'Neill (1888-1953), Clifford Odets (1906-1963), Thornton Wilder (1897-1975), and Arthur Miller (1915-2005). Any inventory is incomplete as the ever-increasing literary talent cannot be strictly numbered and categorized.

This anthology contains 14 essays, which offer a critical insight into the 20th century American literature. The essays investigate multiple themes and authors within the said period. The book contains research papers from researchers in India, Saudi Arabia, Pakistan and Africa.

Rupali Saran Mirza
Assistant Professor.
Department of English.
Integral University.

WORKS CITED

Abbotson, Susan C.W. *Critical Companion to Arthur Miller: A Literary Reference to His Life and Work*. New York: Facts on File Inc. 2007.

Adams, J.T. *The Epic of America*. Garden City, NY: Blue Ribbon Books. 1941.

Beuka, Robert. *American Icon Fitzgerald's 'The Great Gatsby' in Critical and Cultural Context*. Rochester, New York: Camden House, 2011.

Dreiser, Theodore. *Sister Carrie*. The Floating Press. 2009.

Elias, Robert H. *Theodore Dreiser: Apostle of Nature*. New York: Knopf, 1949; revised, Ithaca: Cornell University Press, 1970.

Hobby, Blake. *Bloom's Literary Themes: The American Dream*. New York: Infobase Publishing. 2009.

Kennedy, X.J., Dana Gioia and Mark Bauerlein. *Handbook of Literary Terms: Literature, Language, Theory*. New Delhi: Pearson Education, Inc. 2005.

Contributors

Sadia Riaz and **Rida Sarfraz.** Lecturer, Institute of Communication and Cultural Studies, University of Management and Technology, C-II Johar Town, Lahore (Pakistan).

Houria Ait Ammour. Doctor in American Literature and Civilisation, Department of English, University of Algiers, Algeria.

Sangeeta Sharma. Head, Department of English, Birla College of Arts, Science and Commerce, Kalyan, Maharashtra (India).

Shaista Maseeh. Asst. Professor, Qassim Colleges, Al Qassim, KSA.

Shaharyar Haider. Lecturer, Department of English, GC University, Lahore (Pakistan).

Neena Sharma. Assistant Professor, Raj Kumar Goel Institute of Technology, Ghaziabad, Uttar Pradesh (India).

P. Padma. Associate Professor, Dept. of English, Yogi Vemana University, Andhra Pradesh (India).

Rupali Mirza. Assistant Professor, Department of English, Integral University, Lucknow, Uttar Pradesh (India).

Subashish Bhattacharjee. UGC-Fellow, Department of English, University of North Bengal (India).

Saikat Guha. Research Scholar, Department of English, University of North Bengal, (India).

Anindya Sundar Polley. Ph.D. Research Scholar, Department of English and Foreign Languages. Affiliation: Guru Ghasidas Viswavidyalaya, Bilaspur, Chhattisgarh (India).

Mursalin Jahan. Assistant Professor, Department of English, Integral University, Lucknow, Uttar Pradesh (India).

Lisha Sinha. Research Scholar, Central University of Bilaspur (Guru Ghasidas Viswavidyalaya), Chhattisgarh (India).

Amna Shamim. Assistant Professor, Department of English, Integral University, Lucknow, Uttar Pradesh (India).

Naila Ahmad Suhail. Assistant Professor, Department of English, Integral University, Lucknow, Uttar Pradesh (India).

1

Influence of the Post-depression, Post-World War Scenario: Conflict and Stasis in Eliot's "Prufrock" and Camus's *The Outsider*

Sadia Riaz and *Rida Sarfraz*

ABSTRACT

The advent of the 20th century was greeted by the First and Second World Wars that unveiled man in all his brutality and savagery. It witnessed the loss of man's moral consciousness; loss of belief in religion and religious values. The horrors and the terrors of war stripped mankind from all its illusions of civilization and from all its ideologies of life. Gripped with an overwhelming sense of loss, despair and pessimism, there was a need to come up with new isms and ideologies in order to reach some understanding of the meaning of life. It was thus that "Existentialism" as a philosophical movement emerged. It focused on the plight of the individual man "compelled to assume ultimate responsibility for his acts of free will". Out of this philosophical thought arose "Absurdism" that focused upon the meaninglessness and the irrationality of the world and of man's existence within it." T.S. Eliot's poem, "The Love Song of J. Alfred Prufrock" and Albert Camus's novel, *The Outsider* can be seen as a product of these philosophical movements. The two literary works focus on the existence of man and his place in the meaningless world. This paper attempts to analyze the psyche of the two protagonists: Prufrock in Eliot's poem and Meursault in Camus's novel, as they observe the absurdity of life around them. It will explore the consciousness of these two characters as they act or fail to act in order to bring about some change or realization among the people of their time.

Keywords: Existentialism, Myth of Sysiphus, Degeneration, Absurdism, Apocalyptic World War, Lost generation.

Existentialism

It basically deals with the notion that through an amalgamation of consciousness, free will, and personal liability, one can create their own connotation inside a world that essentially has none of its own. Existential themes such as trepidation, monotony, alienation, the meaningless, freedom, commitment and nothingness. It also refers to the individual being responsible for the actions and decision one makes; without any certain knowledge of what is right or wrong.

Absurdism

It deals with quintessence of the meaningless that implies to a tragic propensity and approach of frustration that emerge out of the hostility between the human pursuit for the purpose of life and its aloofness. Absurdism implies a tragic tone and feelings of frustration that arise out of the contradiction between the human quest for the meaning of life and its inaccessibility. It is the belief that human beings survive in a purposeless, muddled universe. The idea of the absurd is a common theme in many existentialist works, particularly in Camus. Critics of absurdism lean to spotlight on two areas of the philosophy. The first is the proposition, as Camus interprets, that life's absence of meaning seems to eradicate any rationale for living. Camus answers this with methods of living with the absurd: through coping or through upheaval—and by pointing out that this lack of purpose presents humankind with true freedom. Others consider the theory itself to be conceited, stating that although the purpose of life may not be evident, that does not prove that it does not exist.

Discussion

T.S. Eliot's poem, "The Love Song of J. Alfred Prufrock", opens with an aura of complete stasis. His imagery of a "patient etherized upon a table" (Eliot, 1917) denotes the complete inertia of man, who is numbed to the core and suffers from an emotional and intellectual paralysis. The 'saw-dust restaurants' (Eliot, 1917) also denote the moral and intellectual decay of mankind who continue to live in a world where everything is transitory like saw dust. However, it is not merely the streets and the hotels that display the grotesque and pathetic condition of mankind. Rather it is the entire atmosphere which is impregnated with spiritual pollution and a sense of futility and indolence.

Moreover, Eliot goes on to highlight the shallowness of the society, when he criticizes the pretentious attitude of the women as he says "In the room the women come and go.... Talking of Michelangelo" (Eliot, 1917). He points out that human value, human life and human relationships have all lost their value in this world. Man is in fact living a day-to-day existence without realizing the utter meaninglessness of his life and the nothingness in which he dwells.

Camus too creates a similar atmosphere in his novel, *The Outsider*. There, Camus creates his protagonist, Meursault, as one who lives a passive existence, detached from the happenings of the world. The novel beginning with the death of his mother, unveils the hypocrisy of the society who put up a convincing pretense of grief for the loss of his mother. It is Meursault, who observes that "this dead body, lying there among them, didn't mean anything to them" (Camus, 1941). However, as Camus points out, the difference between Meursault and the rest of the world, lies in the fact that Meursault refuses to "play the game" (1941). While Meursault notes the absurd pretense of grief displayed by the people around him, his fault lies in the fact that he fails to show any emotion towards his loss and that he does not portray himself as anything or anyone other than what he really is. His observation of the absurdity of life around him, is something that the reader takes immediate note of, but Meursault remains unconscious of for some part of the novel.

His unconsciousness is, thus, a contrast to the consciousness of Prufrock who is aware of not only the absurdity around him, but also the absurdity within him. Meursault in his detachment is separated from being a part of the absurdity of the world, while Prufrock realizes that he is himself a part of the whole in the absurdity of life. He too, along with the countless members of society, is caught up in creating illusions and masking his true identity; preparing "a face to meet the (other) faces" (Eliot, 1917). It is this that creates the conflict of action and inaction in Prufrock. Being a part of the whole and separated from the whole at the same time, in his consciousness, leads to the fragmentation of Prufrock's character. He experiences a divide within him; an internal dilemma between remaining passive or impassive in the world and among the ignorant people of the world. Desirous of gaining a socially acceptable role, Prufrock is constantly afraid of inviting the disapproval and derision of society. He fears that they will evaluate his emotional and psychological failings, and ridicule his wretched condition:

> And I have known the eyes already, known them all—
>
> The eyes that fix you in a formulated phrase. (Eliot, 1917)

These 'eyes' of the others, strip Prufrock of an individual personality and identity. In order to remain a part of society, he prefers to blind himself to his 'momentary' spiritual awakenings and chooses to remain inactive in bringing about any change in the absurd world.

In contrast to Prufrock's fragmentation, is Camus' character Meursault of *The Outsider*. Meursault, a 'stranger' and an 'outsider': detached and alienated from the world from the very beginning of the novel, does not undergo any dilemma or split in his character. While he remains passive and unconscious of the absurdity of the world for most part of the novel, he is eventually aroused after he commits murder and is subjected to a court trial. Having murdered an Arab man, Meursault realizes that he had "destroyed the balance of the day" and knocked "at the door of unhappiness" (Camus, 1941). Life as he had once lived it changes from here on. However, aware of his guilt in committing murder, what rouses Meursault is not only the awareness of this guilt but also the absurdity of facing a trial. While he perceives his case as "simple enough" (Camus, 1941) with his obvious guilt, the system of law and order nevertheless require him to appoint a lawyer, and to face a trial.

It is, thus, the trial that pursues, and further arouses Meursault's consciousness of the absurdity of the world, when he is questioned more about his lack of feelings towards his mother's death and less about his act of committing murder. Moreover, Meursault's lawyer suggests that he tamper with the real story of committing murder in order to escape his death sentence. In this, his lawyer depicts the common psyche of every man who travels through life and through lying and pretense. Camus writes in the Afterword, "Lying is not only saying what isn't true. It is also in fact especially saying more than is true and, in the case of the human heart, saying more than one feels. We all do it, everyday, to make life simpler" (1941). He also states that it is this refusal to lie that separates Meursault from the world.

Meursault, unhindered by the eye of society, unlike Prufrock is determined not to lie and in this decision he parallels Albert Camus definition of the rebel. Camus explains in his essay, *The Rebel* that:

> In every act of rebellion, the rebel simultaneously experiences a feeling of revulsion at the infringement of his rights and a complete and spontaneous loyalty to certain aspects of himself. Thus he implicitly brings into play a standard of values so far from being gratuitous that he is prepared to support it no matter what the risks. (1956, p. 10)

Meursault, thus, in standing up for his beliefs and in refusing to lie in fact rebels against the system of the world. In protecting his values, he asserts his separation from the absurd world. In order to assert his beliefs, Meursault is prepared to risk the consequences, which in this case, is his death sentence. Sprintzen writes about Meursault's rebellion, commenting on his idea of revolt:

> revolt is not only the metaphysical rejection of social hypocrisy, but also the personal purgation of the temptation

> to play by the rules—even to be the dandy—and the re-affirmation of the individual's right, experienced by Camus almost as a characterological duty, to be witness in one's actions to the truth of one's experience. (2001, 125)

Meursault through this rebellion does not live up to Camus standards of the absurd man as explained in his essay, *The Myth of Sisyphus*. Camus states that the absurd man must be conscious of the absurdity of the world but must not seek to put an end to his life. Rather he must accept it and live on. However, at the same time, Camus does address the concept of 'conquest' in *The Myth of Sisyphus*. He writes: "There always comes a time when one must choose between contemplation and action" (1955, p. 56). While he prefers action, he also goes on to say: "Conquerors know that action is in itself useless. There is but one useful action, that of remaking man and the earth. I shall never remake men. But one must do 'as if" (1955, p. 56). It is this exactly that characterizes Meursault's rebellion and decision to act. In standing up against the absurdity of the world, Meursault asserts his individuality. Though he acknowledges the indifference of the world, yet his action can be seen to have an everlasting impact for he remains steadfast and adamant. The novel ends with Meursault's statement: "... my last wish was that there should be a crowd of spectators at my execution and that they should greet me with cries of hatred" (Camus, 1941).

Thus, Meursault embraces the indifference of the world, and in this embrace he asserts his individuality and establishes himself as a character who is at one with himself, unwavered by the influence of society. In his action and in his rebellion, he rises far above society and social standards in the absurd world. David Sprintzen writes about this commenting:

> A motive, no matter how malevolent, bespeaks an intelligible individual. A motivated act is an intelligible act; its world, a familiar world. To insist upon there being a motive—to insist so unselfconsciously that the possibility that there might not be one does not even arise—while, at the same time, characterizing that motive as the willful rejection of humane sensibilities, here truly is the "best

> of all possible worlds." Presented with a criminal who is metaphysically comprehensible but morally reprehensible, society may, at one and the same time, reaffirm its cosmic drama and purge itself momentarily of any repressed and taboo inclinations that threaten to shatter it.

Meursault's rebellion is in stark contrast to Prufrock's choice to remain inactive and passive. He allows himself to be intimidated by the eye of society. Afraid of being misinterpreted and being ousted from society, Prufrock chooses to play safe and to continue to live on. However, in his failure to act, Prufrock begins to indulge in self-justification. He states:

> I should have been a pair of ragged claws
> Scuttling across the floors of silent seas. (Eliot, 1917)

This degenerated and disembodied image of a crab, that Prufrock desires to be, not only emphasizes upon the disintegration of Prufrock, of the character himself, but also points toward his desire to absolve himself of all responsibilities. Being torn between choosing to mould himself according to the society or bringing the moment of questioning "to its crisis" (Eliot, 1917), he desires to merely become a part of the silent sea, with no defined identity and no responsibilities to live up to. He also goes on to further justify himself stating:

> No! I am no Prince Hamlet, nor was meant to be;
> Am an attendant lord, one that will do
> To swell a progress, start a scene or two. (Eliot, 1917)

A critic by the name of Carol T. Christ writes in an article, that J. Alfred Prufrock "laments his loss while he constructs a fiction of the self that at once rationalizes his failure and consoles him for it.... The accuracy and wit of his social satire and the plangency of his lament for his failure alike afford him defenses against the world he has refused to enter" (1984, pp. 220-21). However, in this battle of self-justification with himself, Prufrock merely establishes his fragmented character. The poem, in contrast with Camus's novel, reaches no conclusion. It begins with images that depict a sense of stasis, inertia and inaction. While initially Eliot depicts the atmosphere of inertia in Prufrock's external surroundings, it is later internalized in Prufrock through his images of himself as a "pair of ragged claws" (Eliot, 1917) and as a mere "attendant lord" (Eliot, 1917). Prufrock thus allows this inertia to dominate him and to desensitize him of his consciousness and of the absurdity of the world.

Thus, in this conflict between action and inaction, Meursault rises above Prufrock. Unhindered and untainted by the influence of society, he is able to stand up for his beliefs and leave his mark in the world. However, Prufrock in his passivity, merely plunges deeper into the absurd world. The contrast between these two protagonists, thereby, vividly depicts the conflict between action and inaction. Prufrock, intimidated by society chooses to remain inactive and the fragmentation of his character becomes evident. Meursault, having confidence in himself and in his decisions, emerges as a character who is at one with himself, and thereby able to assert his individuality.

WORKS CITED

Camus, A. *The Outsider*. London: Everyman's Library. 1941.

Christ, T.C. "Self-Concealment and Self-Expression in Eliot's and Pound's Dramatic Monologues". *Victorian Poetry*, Vol. 22, No. 2, *The Dramatic "I" Poem*, 217-26. 1984.

Eliot, T.S. "The Love Song of J. Alfred Prufrock". Retrieved from: http://www.bartleby.com/198/1.html. L-3, 8, 13-14, 27, 55-56, 73-74, 80, 111-13, 1941.

Sprintzen, D. "The Stranger". In Bloom, H. (Ed.), *Modern Critical Interpretations: Albert Camus's The Stranger* (pp. 107-26). New York: NY, Chelsea House, 1941.

2

Learned Americans in John Dos Passos's *USA*: Between the Power of Morality and the Call of Success and Prestige

Houria Ait Ammour

ABSTRACT

During the first three decades of the 20th century, America concentrated on economic growth, technological development and commercial expansion. Economy boomed and materialism triumphed over idealism. The country was engaged in an orgy of spending, a frenzy of speculation and a dizzy search for pleasure. This entailed the collapse of the Puritan values on which the 'Founding Fathers' built their nation. In his USA trilogy, John Dos Passos expresses his disenchantment regarding this loss of moral values through the behaviour of some learned characters who, after taking part in World War I, decide to give their talents up for the sake of wealth, prestige and power. The present article is concerned with the way some of these learned Americans—mainly Mourehouse, the public counsel and Eléanor and Eveline, the artists—are portrayed. Our aim is to stress on the danger this new class represents for the economy, culture and values of fictional America, notably on its capacity to subvert and pervert, on its neglect of human dignity, political freedom and economic equality and on its devotion to the businessmen's interests at the expense of America's ancient moral code and sacred system of values.

Keywords: USA, Learned American, Artist, Public Counsel, World War One, Capitalism, Prestige, Money.

John Dos Passos's trilogy, *USA*,[1] starts at the beginning of the twentieth century and closes on the eve of the 1929 economic depression. In these three novels, the writer condemns the destruction of the American moral values resulting from the great political, social and ideological changes the country knew after World War I. Some learned characters, mainly the publicist J. Ward Moorehouse, and the artists Eléanor Stoddard and Eveline Hutchins embody these changes. They are educated persons who could have put their knowledge at the service of their people. Instead, they have chosen to give their talents up for the sake of wealth and prestige. In this article, we concentrate on the danger this new class represents for the economy, culture and values of fictional America.

A self-made millionaire, a publicist and labor politician, Moorehouse is a prototype of the ruthless American opportunist. Intellectually, he is not outstanding; he conforms easily to all kinds of myths, be they new or ancient, provided he can get profit from them. He is a kind of parasite, a non-productive person haunted by the idea of joining the upper class by all means. His intellectual/ethical poverty becomes a practical superiority in a society where the notions of "right" and "wrong" are replaced by those of "success" and "failure".

Interestingly, Moorehouse is offered his greatest chance with America's entry into World War I which he sees as an occasion for a better social status even if at the expense of moral values. Now a public relations counsel, 32 years old, prepares himself to the great adventure in his own way. Here starts the decisive operation: the modification of the social structure which Dos Passos wants to denounce. Supposed to pursue moral ends, the public counsel will, however, do his best to neutralize the dreaded trade union opposition and to promote reconciliation between the capitalists and the workers.

The period chosen by Dos Passos is difficult; it is characterized by a rapid growth of trade unions. In addition to the repression of popular forces, a new strategy is applied: dialogue between the leaders of the workers and the representatives of the capitalists (public counsels).

The new type of patronage to whom Moorehouse is the servant consists of elaboration of a new technique of conciliation between employers and employees. A modern American way of life invented by businessmen, monopolies and trusts appears. It aims at preserving the businessmen's interests by carefully engineering their image and, thus, trying to soften the social impact of their harsh politics. And this is Moorehouse's specific duty.

According to Dos Passos, the American Government wanted to prevent the trade unions from being influenced by Marxist ideas which were spreading rapidly among the Wobblies.[2] It thus judged it necessary to explain to the common man that America was an exception. It was impossible to interpret in Marxist terms, with an ideology issued by Europe and suitable for it only a reality and a situation specifically American. Americans had to prove very quickly that the most important point in Marxism—class conflict—could not be accepted in the United States. The theory of natural rights, the principle of equal opportunities for everybody, the dogma of the perfect equality between all the citizens of the "country of God" were specifically American. A class ideology could never be conserved in these old respectable institutions.

The 'public counsels', like Moorehouse, were at the service of the dominant class. It was their duty to convince public opinion that America was totally original: the friendly cooperation between the worker and his boss was very easy. Such propaganda could be rationally organized. Dos Passos recognizes that he has been inspired by Ivy Lee in the creation of Moorehouse.[3] Lee was one of the first leaders of the burgeoning public relations industry that was being advanced by former newspapermen who recognized a new, specialized fact of the press industry.[4] Dos Passos met him in Moscow in 1928 and learnt much on his opinions.[5] Just like Moorehouse, Lee became famous by helping businessmen guilty of bad labor practices benefit from having their views presented correctly to the public. He became more famous—like Moorehouse again—when he served as a publicity director and later an assistant to the chairman of the American Red Cross in World War I. Lee accepted to turn language into a device for the manipulation of public belief and this is what made Dos Passos use him as a prototype. Moorehouse is also a perfect user of words. Among his favorite terms to disguise the injustice toward labor and the public are "cooperation", "understanding" and "education".

Dos Passos accompanies each of Moorehouse's narrative segments by a biography of a person misappropriating the American popular faith or its language. The biography preceding the first narrative segment of Moorehouse is that of "the Silver Tongue of the plain people" (p. 171, William Jennings Bryan, the first secretary of state under President Wilson who misuses his gift of language and propagandises his people). Minor C. Keith, a prototype of the great industrial fortune-standing as a type for the economic imperialism of the twentieth century—is of the same kind: "the Emperor of the Caribbean" exploits the workers for his own interests in the name of the classic "American success myth". Andrew Carnegie, the Scottish-American industrialist and the most important philanthropist of his era, is another example of the people who succeed in masking the truth by honorific public images and language. He was himself at the head of the Bessemer companies, conciliating delicately the demands of Capitalism with those of his legend. All these biographies refer to hypocrites who adopt public roles and use language to disguise their real intentions. That is why Dos Passos inserts them in Moorehouse's segments.

Through such a character, Dos Passos denounces the manipulation and corruption of language. Moorehouse misuses 'words' to protect "the myth of success". All along his life, he does not realize that he is using others to serve his own interests, and he calls this loyalty; when corporations use their employees to their own advantage, he terms this "cooperation" (p. 230). He does not do this on purpose. His belief in this language is so strong that he cannot see the truth. Not only does he have a great faith in the myth of success, he is also endowed with a power to control and to blind. Indeed Moorehouse is important, but his importance is destructive. He stands for the betrayal of the American values, of the sincere "Old Words".

Dos Passos reproaches his characters, not with what they do but rather with how they do it and what they become by doing it. He hates Moorehouse, not because he has cheated the workers by the creation of the labor-relations board, but rather because he uses false words to reach his aim. Likewise G.H. Barrow, the duplicitous labor faker, is presented negatively, not because he betrays labor, but rather for his lies, for his talking about 'the art of living' when he means concupiscence. These two learned characters could have been positive had they not chosen to lie to the people and to put their knowledge at the service of 'Big Business'. What interests Dos Passos is not the usefulness of an action but rather the quality of the person who does it.

On coming back from Europe, this 'modern wizard of publicity' becomes an authentic 'public counsel': he strives hard to show to the common American the place "Big Enterprise" plays in his community and to prove that it works for the happiness and prosperity of all Americans. He insists again on that relation of confident cooperation that should be created between workers and employers, what he calls "the team spirit". He says, "capital and labor those two great forces of our national life neither of which can exist without the other are growing further apart" (p. 229).

Once again, Dos Passos bases his narrative on an exact documentation, on social and economic realities. Each rise in the prices of the U.S. steel, for example, is preceded by a rigorous psychological preparation which shows that society is working for the common good and is acting according to law and justice. Now with Moorehouse, the American dream is being realized, thanks to American Capitalism and to the devotion of the monopolies. Nevertheless, it efficiently neutralizes the dangerous activities of the Wobblies and attributes all the achievements realized by the Unions to the Trusts. This is the new science of public counselling, and also one of the methods of American Capitalism.

Moorehouse, in a conference with Judge Bowie Planet, a minor character who incarnates law but is in fact a horrible speculator, and Mr. Barrow, a former secretary of the Brotherhood of Locomotive Engineers (the working world), now at the service of the businessmen, exposes his views. He wants to create an agency destined to solve the conflicts between the workers and their employers in a friendly way. "I've rarely heard a businessman speak with such sympathy and understanding of the labor situation", says Judge Planet to Moorehouse (p. 230). It is important to establish contact with the working class without alarming them. The period is propitious, "this war in Europe [...] is America's great opportunity", says Barrow (p. 230). Moorehouse's solution to the conflict between employers and employees will be exposed the day after during a rotary lunch: to educate the public is an urgent necessity; both employers and employees should serve the public; the workers will be included in the world of 'Big Business'; they will be given some shares at low prices; they will be accomplices without, however, including them in the intended immense profits. Only in this way will the dangers of Socialism and demagoguery be avoided. In this case, an education campaign is necessary to build a public opinion (p. 231).

Moorehouse' ascension is a cruel satire of the naivety of the American individual. Through him, Dos Passos condemns the behavior of the 'Trusts' responsible for this artificial way of life as well as for the wars from which they live. He never mentions the industrialists directly; he keeps alluding to them through Moorehouse who is no more than their servant. Through this character, Dos Passos underlines the dominant pattern of American society. Moorehouse carries along with him his platonic mistress Eleanord and her friend Eveline. These women[6] are interesting because, being learned, like Moorehouse, they could have become intellectuals—like the Greenwich Village women of that time—had they not been blinded by money.

Undoubtedly, the American society Dos Passos depicts was a sexist one: history shows that in the field of labor disputes, big business and war, women were nearly completely absent.[7] Their presence in the Newsreels testifies to their inferior and debased social status. They do not participate in politics and business; independence for them is restricted to dressing and courtship. They are objectified, minimized (see Newsreels 11 and 12 in *The 42nd Parallel*).

As to Dos Passos's learned females, they are no better. Most of them succumb to money, prestige or power. Eleanor is an artist, but she never fulfils her duties in her society as such. An artist is supposed to take a stand in his society. Eleanor is utterly passive: she never comments on the events happening around her—at least in the name of universal ethics as artists do; she does not contest the socio-political situation of America in such an agitated period, nor does she oppose the capitalists' exploitation of the workers. Though she decides to take part in World War I by going to France as a nurse, she never tries to understand the reasons for such a war. She is a typical uncommitted educated woman unable to make up her mind politically and culturally. Dos Passos depicts her cruelly to punish her for such an attitude.

Her inherited pseudo culture constitutes an important challenge for her as a genteel woman. It prevents her from adapting to modern life. She is frozen, relentless, ruthless, a kind of "mort vivante". She is the most tragic character of the trilogy. Her world changes according to exterior impulsions because it has no lasting values. She moves from aestheticism to the practical job of interior decorator to gain more money.

Eléanor's aspiration for ascendancy makes her lose her value as a respected intellectual who used to appreciate arts. In *The Big Money*, she is still that selfish woman we left in the *42nd Parallel* and *1919*. Now—more than ever before—she betrays Democracy, loses the notion of ideological commitment and abandons completely her artistic career to enter the world of business and to seek for a better lifestyle. She becomes Moorehouse's associate in his striving to belong to the 'leisure class'.

By the end of the novel, she, who used to identify with Moorehouse, the capitalist, is depicted organizing a great party in which she invites wealthy people and a group of "émigrée Russians in tiaras" (p. 1124) and offers them a great banquet with Caviar and Salmon (p. 1126). Eléanor lights candles near an icon (p. 1125) and offers her guests tea in "Silver Samovar" (p. 1125). Now that "she is filthy with money" (p. 1124), as Eveline her friend says, she has the right to belong to the 'Leisure Class', especially after she has decided to marry the Russian prince Mingraziali (p. 1127). Capitalism and socialism no longer mean anything to her.

Eveline is another interior decorator who falls victim to 'the machine'. Like her friend Eléanor, she appears to be a sophisticated woman with a refined literary and artistic culture. Indeed, early in her life, she is endowed with an artistic talent and a passion for the poetry and art of the pre-Raphaelite Brotherhood. Later, she is even involved in radical politics when she gets acquainted with the Communist painter Don Stevens. But this is only a façade behind which hides a woman devoid of any commitment to human values. Her life is dominated by social relations in which she mixes feelings with business. She now belongs to 'the Leisure Class'. She keeps organizing parties in which she invites society people who come to exhibit their wealth and waste their time drinking, smoking and laughing (p. 1175). She sacrifices her inward life, her artistic capacities for money and social approval. She alienates herself from the area she grew in to seek for a better style of living. She fails in whatever she undertakes and her boredom with this habit of failure leads her to suicide, a form of punishment on the part of Dos Passos.

Like many American women of the 1920s, she is obsessed with sex. She confuses it with experimental/immoral art: she poses nude for an artist who seduces her. She marries the innocent Paul Johnson because he has impregnated her, while she, at the same time, is engaged to many other men.

Dos Passos is disappointed with the behaviour of Eléanor and Eveline; he would have liked them to remain clean artists, to put their art at the service of their nation. This disappointment takes him back to the past and to compare Eléanor to the famous American architect Frank Lloyd Wright to ascertain the process of the degradation of U.S. art. The biographical portrait he draws of Wright is that of the greatest interior designer and educator of his time who devoted his life to designing structures which were in harmony with humanity and its environment.

Moorehouse, Eléanor and Eveline vacillate between modern life and the badly protected debris of their old culture. Consequently, they adopt a new confused attitude characterized by frustration, cynicism and ambition: they accept the new norms of success easily because of the weakness of their own values. They never indulge in thinking as learned people. They care about nothing except their desires and appetites. Living in a world with no moral concern, they are not affected by any moral values. Nothing stimulates them; that is why they can be neither memorable nor individually significant. Consequently, the reader in search of intellectual suggestion cannot identify with them; nor can he be touched by their lives.

The hunger for power, wealth, influence and success prevents these characters from reflecting on what is happening around them or at least on their fates. Moreover, the dehumanization of the modern American society which came as a consequence of rapid technological improvements and industrial modernization prevents them from acting as learned people. They are automata. Moorehouse could have exploited the high social position he reached more positively. He could have contributed to the well-being of the American people in general—not to that of the big businessmen only. He had all the possibilities for that: money, intelligence and social status. Nothing obliged him to betray the old American values. Eléanor and Eveline could have devoted their artistic abilities to the service of the masses instead of turning them into a mere source of income. These characters are un-American because their words and actions betray and deny the "Old Words" on which the Founding Fathers built their democratic America. That is why the writer punishes them severely: some are killed, others are destroyed economically and some others end up with moral breakdown.

END NOTES

1. John Dos Passos, *USA* (London: Penguin, 1966). *The 42nd Parallel* was published in 1930, 1919 in 1932 and *The Big Money* in 1936. But they have been put in a single volume in 1938 by Penguin Books. All future references to these novels will be taken from this edition and page references will be put between parentheses and inserted in the text.
2. On the Wobblies or IWW (Industrial Workers of the World) see Melvyn Dubofsky, *We Shall Be All: A History of the Industrial Workers of the World* (Illinois: University of Illinois Press, 2000).
3. Donald Pizer, *Dos Passos's USA* (Charlotte Ville: University Press of Virginia, 1988), p. 118.
4. Ray Eldon Robert, *Courtier to the Ground: The Story of Ivy Lee and the Development of Public Relations* (Ames: Lowa State University Press, 1966).
5. Pizer, *op. cit.*, p. 126.
6. On women in Dos Passos see Janet Galligani Casey, *Dos Passos and the Ideology of the Feminine* (Cambridge: Cambridge University Press, 1988).
7. Janet Galligani Casey, "Historicizing the Female in *USA*. Re-Vision of Dos Passos's Trilogy", *Twentieth Century Literature*, 41, 3 (Autumn, 1995), 249-65.

WORKS CITED

Casey, Janet Gallighani. *Dos Passos and the Ideology of the Feminine*. Cambridge: Cambridge University Press, 1988.

Casey, Janet Gallighani. "Historicizing the Female in U.S.A.: Revision of Dos Passos's Trilogy". *Twentieth Century Literature*. 1995.

Dubofsky, Melvyn. *We Shall Be All: A History of the Industrial Workers of the World*. Illinois: University of Illinois Press, 2000.

Passos, John Dos. *The 42nd Parallel*. London: Penguin, 1966.

Pizer, Donald. *Don Passos's U.S.A. Charlotte Ville*: University Press of Virginia, 1988.

3

Languishing at the Periphery: Arthur Miller's Women Characters

Sangeeta Sharma

ABSTRACT

Death of a Salesman (1949) occupies a central position in the *oeuvre* of Arthur Miller. The subtitle of the play is: *Certain Private Conversations in Two Acts and a Requiem*. It is a play that has gained international critical acclaim and great commercial success. *Death of a Salesman* is a fine example of Miller's craftsmanship and view of the post-Depression American society. Miller is at his creative best in this hard-hitting play, generally regarded as the critique of the American Dream. Miller's leftist orientation and the Ibsenesque influence are on display in this domestic drama of American life. The protagonist is Willy Loman, a salesman, now in his sixties, who gradually feels redundant in a commodity economy, with decreasing exchange value in the reified social system.

Much has been written about the ordinariness of the salesman, Willy Loman, the central character of the play and his declining ability to sell commodities in the market. Basically, it is a masculine play that deals with values like aggression, competition and sexual domination deeply inscribed in the capitalist patriarchal American system. Despite his finer sensibilities and humanist concerns, Arthur Miller fails to give primary importance to female characters in his plays, including the *Death of a Salesman.* Most of these females have internalized the value-orientation of the patriarchy and, therefore, try desperately to conform to the ideal roles of a mother, sister, daughter and a housewife. They dutifully carry out the demands made on them by the patriarchy and sacrifice their own personalities in this process. The women characters in the theatrical world of Arthur Miller are always on the margins and content to be there. There is no private space or individual growth as human beings for them. This is a surprising discovery because Miller happens to be a Marxist and quite objective in his approach towards society of his time. Any gender study of Miller's major plays can easily attest to the marginalisation of women. This lack of progressive attitude towards women, perhaps, is indicative of the deep entrenchment and implication of Miller in the contemporary society of the 40s, 50s and 60s that treated women as no more than domestic slaves or as sex dolls.

The present gender-study of Miller's *Death of a Salesman* attempts a revaluation of his male-driven world view from a feminist point of view. It seeks to establish the fact that Miller, despite his progressive outlook, remains a male chronicler of his times and fails to produce memorable female characters that can match a Willy Loman, Proctor, Joe Keller, etc. in terms of popularity and depth. The women in plays like *Death of a Salesman, The Crucible* or *All My Sons*—to name only a few—are highly domesticated and mere shadows of the powerful male protagonists.

Keywords: Marginalization, Patriarch/y/chal, Entrenched, ideal/ised, Dreams.

Death of a Salesman portrays a typical middle-class American home of the 1940s where a man goes out to work and chases the American dream of success, and, his woman works as a homemaker. The whole play revolves around the pathetic figure of Willy Loman and his falling value in a society where youth and appearances count a lot. Matthew C. Roudane, in his essay observes:

> *Death of a Salesman* is a deceptively simple play. Its plot revolves around the last twenty-four hours in the life of Willy Loman, the hard-working sixty-three year old travelling salesman whose ideas of professional, public success jar with the realities of his private desires and modest accomplishments. (Bigsby, 60)[1]

The action is set in New York and Boston of the day. In Act I, Miller in the stage instructions, describes the salesman's house and Willy Loman, the salesman, and Linda, his wife in vivid terms. Willy Loman is past sixty years of age and visibly exhausted. Describing Linda, Miller writes:

> Linda, his wife, has stirred in her bed at the right. She gets out and puts on a robe, listening. Most often jovial, she has developed an iron repression of her exceptions to Willy's behaviour—she more than loves him, she admires him, as though his mercurial nature, his temper, his massive dreams and little cruelties, served her only as sharp reminders of the turbulent longings within him, longings which she shares but lacks the temperament to utter and follow to their end. (I, 131)

This paragraph reveals the character of Linda as a typical homemaker. Whereas the earlier paragraph of the stage instructions, Loman is described in a loving manner, with details about his age and physical state given clearly, the same is missing about his wife. Neither her age is mentioned nor her physical state of wellness is mentioned. In the paragraph cited above, only a brief sketch of Linda emerges. Over the years, she has come to mould herself and accept Willy Loman's shortcomings in a housewifely manner. This is suggested by the word 'iron repression'. Iron repression is a key term here that underlies the repression of women in the domestic milieu. It is a psychological way of making suitable adjustments with the grim realities of marriage and home. Through repression of their natural feelings and natural self, women tend to modify their behaviour and adopt a passive attitude by which they conform to the harsh demands of patriarchy and its rigid stereotypes.

The opening act itself is revealing about the status of these two persons in the domestic sphere. The scene opens with Linda showing her genuine concern for her husband and husband feeling irritated by this concern. Willy Loman shows his rough side in the following dialogue:

> LINDA, *hearing Willy outside the bedroom, calls with some trepidation:* Willy!
>
> WILLY: It's all right. I came back.
>
> LINDA: Why? What happened? *Slight pause.* Did something happen, Willy?
>
> WILLY: No, nothing happened.
>
> LINDA: You didn't smash the car, did you?
>
> WILLY, *with casual irritation*: I said nothing happened. Didn't you hear me?
>
> LINDA: Don't you feel well?
>
> WILLY: I'm tired to the death. *The flute has faded away. He sits on the bed beside her, a little numb*. I couldn't make it. I just couldn't make it, Linda.
>
> LINDA, *very carefully, delicately*: Where were you all day? You look terrible. (I, 131)

This domestic scene is built upon the traditional notions of male as a pampered breadwinner and female as a subservient thing, out to humour the master of the house. In this exchange of dialogues, the character of Linda acts out the role of a dutiful, obedient, caring, self-effacing wife to the hilt. Later in the scene, Linda is shown taking off his shoes. While Willy has a dominating and dismissive attitude towards her, his wife of many years uses all the endearments to soothe him, calling the salesman 'dear' repeatedly. In the subsequent dialogues, Willy Loman is shown to be brash, angry and loud, while discussing their son Biff. Linda, on the other hand, is gentle, polite, soothing and explanatory. She wants to comfort him and uses placatory language. She is infinitely patient and caring for both her husband and son, playing the role of a peacemaker. Miller repeatedly stresses this tender side, the mothering side of a female in the directions and in the pithy dialogues between her and her husband whereas Willy Loman calls his wife, a few minutes after the opening of the play, as his foundation and support and his anchor (I, 135).

This is the only time when he makes this concession to this long suffering and self-effacing wife. The repetition of *my* in such a short one-line sentence is significant. It implies Willy's acknowledgement of the multiple roles played by Linda in his life and their family. *Foundation* and *support* mutually reinforce each other and suggest the image of a structure. Structure that has a solid base and a supporting system. Linda as a married woman provides this solid foundation to the structure of the family that is headed by the husband, followed by her two sons in terms of power and importance. The domestic hierarchy and the distribution of power solely revolve around the patriarch and the male descendants. In such a hierarchy, the role of a wife and a mother is relegated to the bottom. The words 'my foundation' and 'my support' demonstrate patriarchy's attitude towards women, whose job is to provide physical and emotional relief to the men. She is subservient to husband Willy Loman; a negotiator between father and his sons, and, is an assertive mother. She is always pleading the case of Willy Loman with her sons and trying to impress them with the greatness of this American father, who could not realize his dream of success and big money, and, who in his old age, finds himself redundant and a failure.

Linda tries to change the hostile attitude of Biff towards his father by asking them: "Why are you so hateful to each other? Why is that?" (I, 161).

Linda plays the dual role of a doting wife and a mother:

> *With a threat, but only a threat, of tears*: He's the dearest man in the world to me, and I won't have anyone making him feel unwanted and low and blue. You've got to make up your mind now, darling, there's no leeway any more. Either he's your father and you pay him that respect, or else you're not to come here. I know he's not easy to get along with—nobody knows that better than me—but.... (I, 162)

Motherhood is also extolled in the play. The sons, more or less admire her, if not exactly worship her.

The following scene amply illustrates their attitude towards their mother, Linda. This scene operates at two levels. Willy is discussing the dress code with Biff for a possible meeting with Oliver, a businessman. Willy is also giving some tips about this meeting. He asks Biff to talk less in order to please Oliver. Linda, as usual, intervenes in the conversation by adding her observations. Willy, the impatient husband, does not like this. He shouts at her, which provokes their son. At one level, it shows her husband's domineering attitude and at another level, it shows a son's reverence towards the same woman who is his mother. In a subtle way, the sexual politics in the domestic sphere is laid bare.

The angry showdown between Willy and Biff shows the sexual politics in a middleclass home. Willy, while giving a piece of mind to his son, feels annoyed when interrupted by Linda's comments. In this scene, he pointedly asks Linda: "Will you let me talk?"

At this point, Biff asks Willy not to shout at Linda? This prompts Willy to ask this question: "What're you, takin' over this house?"

Linda again tries to pacify him but Willy flares up and shouts at her, asking her not to take her son's side all the time.

His cursing language, his sudden angry moods, his question, what're you, takin' over this house? reveal the well-entrenched patriarchal values.

Biff, who is straight-forward and blunt, does not like the way his mother is treated by his father. He also questions the authority of his father. This leads to a conflict situation in the domestic realm. Willy Loman does not like this idea of being challenged by his sons. He wants full respect and obedience both from his wife and sons. He believes in the family hierarchy where father as the breadwinner is the head of the family and deserves compliance, complete obedience and loyalty. The family unit reflects the society where these norms of authority and obedience operate at macro level. Conformism and obedience to authority and male gender are necessary for the survival of this kind of unequal capitalist society.

Linda's behaviour in this scene is very typical of a devoted and subservient wife. Although yelled at and even rebuked strongly by her husband, she never feels insulted, disappointed or hurt. She does not mind her *unequal* status in the family. She does not answer back or fight with her husband. She is extremely sweet and caring for Willy Loman. In fact, she is shown to be more articulate than Willy Loman and she becomes a kind of lawyer for the pathetic salesman. Her dialogue supports this contention. She tells Willy that her *pyjamas* are hanging in the bathroom. This caring attitude towards the personal details of her husband combined with an earlier pleading with Biff for a better treatment of Willy by her son makes Happy exclaim in admiration, "What a woman! They broke the mold when they made her."

This leads Biff to say, "She got grey. Mom got awful old."

Both the sons admire their mother and are concerned for her. But Biff is more concerned. He notices his greying mother but fails to see an equally ageing father. He stands up for his quiet self-effacing mother who is totally devoted to his father. He fights with his father for her sake and gets scolded by Linda for this gesture. Linda wants her sons, especially Biff, to understand his father and show love and respect for him. In an earlier scene, Biff says that Willy Loman is a fake. This observation makes Linda angry to the point where she says that he should choose somebody else as his father: "Then make Charlie your father, Biff." The whole dialogue where she defends her husband is worth reproducing here because it shows Linda as an extremely devoted wife:

> LINDA: Then make Charley your father, Biff. You can't do that, can you? I don't say he's a great man. Willy Loman never made a lot of money. His name was never in the paper. He's not the finest character that ever lived. But he's a human being, and a terrible thing is happening to him. So attention must be paid. He's not to be allowed to fall into his grave like an old dog. Attention, attention must be finally paid to such a person. You called him crazy—

BIFF: I didn't mean—

LINDA: No, a lot of people think he's lost his—balance. But you don't have to be very smart to know what his trouble is. The man is exhausted.

HAPPY: Sure!

LINDA: A small man can be just as exhausted as a great man. He works for a company thirty-six years this March, opens up heard-of territories to their trademark, and now in his old age they take his salary away. (I, 162-63)

The character of Linda has been thoroughly idealized by Miller. It fits into the prevalent notions of the 40s and 50s about the feminine and the role of women as homemakers.

Linda is always praising and admiring her husband. She has accepted him in the most uncritical manner. At one point, she calls him as the handsomest man in the world. When Willy protests, she repeats: "To me you are. *Slight pause.* The handsomest" (I, 149).

This prompts Willy to say that she is the best and a friend for him: "You're the best there is Linda, you're a pal, you know that? On the road—on the road I want to grab you sometimes and just kiss the life outa you"(I, 149).

Later on, Linda says fiercely to her sons that Willy is the most precious person in her life and she won't allow anybody to make him feel small. Here she acts as a devoted wife and a protector of the salesman. Her caring attitude and devotion almost border on the motherly love and affection for her ageing husband:

LINDA: Biff, dear, if you don't have any feeling for him, then you can't have any feeling for me.

BIFF: Sure I can, Mom.

LINDA: No. You can't just come to see me, because I love him. *With a threat, but only a threat, of tears*: He's the dearest man in the world to me, and I won't have anyone making him feel unwanted and low and blue. You've got to makeup your mind now, darling, there's no leeway any more. Either he's your father and you pay him that respect, or else you're not to come here. I know he's not easy to get along with—nobody knows that better than me—but...." (I, 162)

Later on, in the play, Linda, in order to comfort Willy also sings a lullaby to him. And after that asks him, "What Biff has got against him". Willy immediately changes his tone, and says, "I'm so tired. Don't talk anymore." This contrast is again revealing of the power politics in the family. Linda wants to comfort him and even sings a song. But Willy, suffering from mood swings, terminates the conversation with his wife and orders her not to talk. The master and slave relationship is quite evident between a dominating husband and a submissive wife.

Linda Loman is shown to possess all the qualities of a good housewife and a good dutiful mother. Miller has portrayed her as per the patriarchal notions about femininity and feminine. By idealizing her as a perfect woman, he tacitly endorses the grim patriarchal system that turns sensitive women into the care-providers of the male members of the society. Their job is to provide physical, mental and emotional comfort to their husbands. In a way, they are slaves of their husbands and don't have any autonomy, financial independence or any say in the running of the family. They have just to follow their husbands and accept their verdicts in an unquestioning manner.

Both as mothers and housewives, women, in Miller, fare better than as girlfriends or mistresses. The attitude of the Lomans—both Willy and his sons—towards other women is very sexist. While Willy Loman is shown to have a brief encounter with a mystery woman, his sons have a very casual and low attitude towards neighbourhood girls.

The following scene vividly describes this extra-marital affair, this brief entanglement of Willy Loman with another woman, despite the devotion and dedication of his legally-wedded wife. Nowhere Willy Loman shows any remorse for this kind of relationship outside the marriage. Both the women are mere objects for him. The woman from Boston openly says that it is she who has picked him up. The kind of passion, Willy shows for her is lacking in the relationship with his wife. The woman thanks him for the stockings presented by him.

She also says that they had a good time together. This memory scene shows that Willy Loman and the woman from Boston have a casual approach towards the sacredness of the institution of the family. On his visits to different cities, a tired unsuccessful Willy does not have anybody to talk to. Low in spirits, he gets picked up by this equally-bored woman and they have a good time together, erasing the earlier identities. They are just interested in having a good time only and using each other for this purpose.

The contrast between the woman and Linda Loman is equally remarkable. The woman says that her sisters would be scandalized if they came to know about having a fling with a travelling salesman. She promises to meet her lover again after two weeks at the same place. Linda, on the other hand, is just the opposite by contrast. She is shown as an idealized version of the female. Nowhere she complains and plays the ideal woman, always defending every action of Willy before her sons or brother-in-law, Ben and friends like Charlie. It appears that Linda's character and intuitive understanding of her husband and his feelings finely balance the crudities of Willy, the salesman, the father, the husband, the friend, and the employee. In a way, she is constructed as a foil to Willy Loman. She becomes the spokesperson of the playwright and provides a perspective on the American culture and life. It seems that Arthur Miller is suggesting that women tend to have a better understanding based on their intuition of their culture and male behaviour.

She is not mesmerized by the successes of Ben Loman. As a woman, she has to perform various roles and tread a fine line. Her character is more complex, strong and well-nuanced than Willy Loman's. In some ways, she reminds readers of Portia or other strong heroines of Shakespeare's comedies. Miller was writing in the 50s. At that historical moment, the Linda Lomans of American middle-class had very few choices. Female liberation was yet to take place. Women were not a part of corporate America. Their role was limited to the domestic sphere, to the kitchen. Playing a dutiful, obedient wife and a good mother was a much common cultural expectation and the Lindas' wonderfully conformed to this stereotyping. They had no other choice. With no economic independence and very few divorce options, they suffered silently.

The most crucial scene comes in Act II where Linda expects a happy family reunion of Willy Loman with his two sons at a local restaurant. It leads to the climax of the play. The meeting of the sons with the father ends unhappily.

Happy asks Biff if he is interested in the girl at the restaurant but he does not seem to be interested. This prompts Happy to say, "Where is your old confidence, Biff?" Biff is not immediately interested but Happy persists, "Do you want her? She is on call." This brief conversation underlines the attitude of the young Lomans towards women. For them they are nothing but mere objects. Sometime later, Willy Loman joins them. He asks Biff about the good news:

> WILLY: I was fired, and I'm looking for a little good news to tell your mother, because the woman has waited and the woman has suffered. The gist of it is that I haven't got a story left in my head, Biff. So don't give me a lecture about facts and aspects. I am not interested. Now what've you got to say to me? (II, 199)

This assessment of Linda by her husband confirms her plight in the house. He says that the woman has waited and the woman has suffered. In a way, it shows the tragedy of the woman in the American household. She has to suffer a lot of inequalities and frustrating experiences that can push her to the margins of the society. The dialogue between Biff and his father is not very productive. There is an ugly confrontation between a disillusioned son and a father. The boys try to cheer him up but fail. They almost come to fight, Willy and Biff. Willy strikes Biff and says, "You rotten little louse! Are you spiting me?" At this point, Happy separates them. Willy, in his mind, goes back to his past where he can hear his mistress laughing. He feels totally disoriented and distracted. Biff takes him to the washroom and leaves him there. Later on, both the sons leave with the girls. When one of the girls, Letta says to Happy that would he not inform his father, Happy replies in the negative. He says, "No, he is not my father. He is just a guy." This denial of the father and abandoning him in the restaurant is cruel gesture on the part of his sons. In the same scene, Willy Loman goes back to his past where he meets that mistress called "The Woman". The scene is almost Freudian in its nature. Arthur Miller reveals that Biff finds his father and the mistress in his hotel room in Boston.

This part of the scene shows that Arthur Miller as a playwright is working on the traditional stereotypes of the women that freely circulate in a patriarchal society and unable to move beyond these notions about women and their sexuality. Linda is shown to be a very patient, caring and loving wife who bears an impeccable moral character, never transgressing the moral boundaries of a wife. Whereas the Woman later identified as Miss Francis, is portrayed as greedy and without scruples, who can give sexual favours for things like stockings. It appears that both Linda and Miss Francis are extremely portrayed in the play. The one is deified, the other is demonized. Miller is operating on the prevalent popular cultural images of the women in this otherwise remarkable play of his, a play that is basically masculine in its plot and focus. The women play a *subordinate* role to the males. Biff, unable to reconcile this shocking discovery of his father's transgression with the earlier image of an ideal father, feels totally shattered and at loss in the wicked adult world where even sacred human emotions are for sale. This realization shakes him to his core. He suddenly loses his faith in the ideals of a family, father and marriage and loses his innocence. This, perhaps, accounts for his later estrangement with his father and all the values his father stands for. He starts drifting away from his family and father.

This probably explains the psychological reason for Biff's adult rebellion against any kind of authority or father figure. This early disillusionment with the system that is morally deficient makes Biff Loman a permanent wanderer and a person who cannot hold a job for long. He is an insider who has understood the duplicity of the moral value system and he has come to reject it. Biff Loman knows the real character of Willy Loman and finds him amoral as a husband who is cheating on his long-suffering mother. The double standards and the hypocrisy are not acceptable to Biff. For the sake of appearances, Biff does not share this little secret with his mother.

In a way, the *Death of Salesman* is a powerful play that delineates the decline of an ageing man who refuses to accept the limiting circumstances of his middle-class life and also the ordinariness of his condition. It also shows the extreme representation of women. The women are portrayed either as long-suffering dutiful wives and mothers or as seductive sirens or mere sex objects in the male universe of Miller. Coming from an enlightened playwright with a heightened sense of morality and social conscience, a famous playwright influenced by the great Henrik Ibsen, the Greeks and the Jewish traditions, this comes as a sad literary shock to the readers and the audiences. It demonstrates the fact that, despite his elevated stature as the moral conscience of America, Miller fails to transcend the oppressive values of the patriarchy and remains deeply embedded in this culture that tends to deny women an equal status and suppresses them. This sexist culture enforces stereotypes on the female gender and ensures a meek conformism and utter obedience from them. In fact, despite advanced capitalism and human rights, women are not more than second citizens, and emancipated writers like Miller, basically remain an organic part to this ideology of suppression.

NOTE

1. Quoted by Matthew C. Roudane, in his essay, "*Death of a Salesman* and the Poetics of ArthurMiller," in Christopher Bigsby (ed.) *The Cambridge Companion to Arthur Miller.* Cambridge: Cambridge University Press, 2000.

WORKS CITED

Carson, Neil. Arthur Miller. London: Macmillan, 1982.

Roudane, C. Matthew. "Death of a Salesman and the poetics of Arthur Miller". The Cambridge Companion to Arthur Miller: Ed. Christopher Bigsby. Cambridge: Cambridge University Press, 1997.

4

'The Roots are as Important as the Wings': *Tar Baby* and African-American Identity in America

Shaista Maseeh

ABSTRACT

Tar Baby, Toni Morrison's fourth novel, was on the *New York Times* best-seller list for four months. It explores themes such as the relationships between men and women, blacks and whites, parents and children, and upper and lower classes of American society. But most of all and most importantly it focuses on the rather complex and delicate relationship between black men and progressive black women. Besides these, various other issues of African-American life are also discussed by Toni Morrison in her own inimitable style.

The narrative of *Tar Baby* is set on a small Caribbean island, in a vacation home, L'Arbe de la Croix, of a retired Philadelphia candy businessman, a white man Valerian Street and his beautiful wife, Margaret Street. They live in this vacation home with Sydney, their black butler and his wife Ondine Childs, the cook, and with Jadine, a black fashion model and niece of Ondine. Son, a young black man on the run arrives in the house and disrupts the peaceful world of L'Arbe de la Croix. Jadine falls in love with Son. Their relationship ends in failure due to the difference in their perspectives of life.

The novel is written in the wake of the Black Feminists Movement of the later 1970s and the 1980s. Morrison brings the elements related to black women in the allegory and the story becomes a complex discussion about the new black woman and her roles and responsibilities vis-a-vis black culture and history.

Keywords: Black history, Culture, Black women, Black feminism, Race, Past.

Tar Baby, Toni Morrison's fourth novel, was on the *New York Times* best-seller list for four months. It explores themes such as the relationships between men and women, blacks and whites, parents and children, and upper and lower classes of American society. But most of all and most importantly it focuses on the rather complex and delicate relationship between black men and progressive black women. Besides these, various other issues of African-American life are also discussed by Toni Morrison in her own inimitable style.

The narrative of *Tar Baby* is set on a small Caribbean island, in a vacation home, L'Arbe de la Croix, of a retired Philadelphia candy businessman, a white man Valerian Street and his beautiful wife, Margaret Street. They live in this vacation home with Sydney, their black butler and his wife Ondine Childs, the cook, and with Jadine, a black fashion model and niece of Ondine. Son, a young black man on the run arrives in the house and disrupts the peaceful world of L'Arbe de la Croix. Jadine falls in love with Son. Their relationship ends in failure due to the difference in their perspectives of life.

The novel centers around the folk image of the Tar Baby, derived from Joel Chandler Harris's Uncle Remus tales, "Tar Baby". Harris's story consists of Br'er Fox who wants to catch Br'er Rabbit. He constructs a sticky tar human figure to trap the rabbit. Br'er Rabbit encounters tar baby but is somehow able to escape from it. The tale has been interpreted as an allegory of slave life where the Rabbit represents the black slave, and the fox the cunning white master who lures the black man to his white world.

Being a black feminist, Morrison sees Tar Baby and 'tar' in her own way. She explains:

> I found that there is a tar baby in African myth. I started thinking about tar. At one point, a tar pit was a holy place, because tar was used to build things. It came naturally out of the earth; it held together things like Moses's little boat and the pyramids. For me, the tar baby came to mean the black woman who can hold things together.[1]

The novel is written in the wake of the Black Feminists Movement of the later 1970s and the 1980s. Morrison brings the elements related to black women in the allegory and the story becomes a complex discussion about the new black woman and her roles and responsibilities vis-à-vis black culture and history.

Jadine: Not Morrison's Tar Baby

As mentioned earlier, Morrison's feminism is one that is closely affiliated to black culture, history, the ancient properties, roots and ethnic values. She doesn't advocate independence that distances itself from the historical and painful 'past'. Her characters such as Claudia in *The Bluest Eye*, Eva in *Sula* and Pilate in *Song of Solomon*, are the preservers of traditional values of the black community and black womanhood. They are like "tar" with their ability to hold families and households together. However, Jadine, the protagonist of *Tar Baby*, is unlike these women.

Jadine defies the conventions of black womanhood. She has a graduate degree from the Sorbonne and she is also a successful model who has been photographed for *Elle* magazine. Apart from that she is also mentored by a rich white man. So, by white standards, she is a liberated woman. But there is a restlessness about her which comes from the fact that she is unsure about her identity. "But for black women, Morrison suggests, and perhaps for all women whose ethnic group and culture have been discriminated by a larger society, 'liberation' must not bring with it alienation from ethnic community."[2] But Jadine is conditioned by Valerian Street and under his influence she becomes distanced from her mother tongue and roots. Barbara Hill Rigney opines that she is "'an art object', a photographer's model who once graced the cover of *Elle* magazine, a white fantasy blackness, and a parody of African art-diluted and, depleted."[3] Jadine is split between the black and the white world. Her two names, Jade and Jadine, exemplify her split identity as she is Jadine to her black aunt and uncle but Jade for the white Street family. She seems to be one of those black people who have been discussed by Carter G. Woodson's in *Miseducation of the Negroes*. Woodson says that "the education of any people should begin with the people themselves, but Negroes...have been dreaming about the ancients of Europe and about those who have tried to imitate them."[4] The fact that she is interested in and values Picasso's work over original Itumba masks indicates her alienation from her own community. Michael, son of Valerian Street, reproves her for abandoning her history and her people. Reporting her conversation with Michael to Valerian, she says:

> I knew what I was leaving.... But he did make me want to apologize for what I was doing, for what I felt. For liking 'Ave Maria' better than gospel music.... Picasso is better than an Itumba mask. The fact that he was intrigued by them is proof of his genius, not the mask makers'.[5]

In three different encounters with traditional black women Jadine's awkwardness and her alienation is underscored. In the first one, she encounters a woman in yellow in a supermarket in Paris. That black woman seems to her so confident of her blackness that, "along with everybody else in the market, Jadine gasped. Just a little.... Just a quick snatch of breath before that woman's woman-that mother/sister/she; that unphotographic beauty-took it all away."[6] But this woman spits at Jadine showing her disapproval for a refined, educated but rootless black model. That woman made her feel "lonely and inauthentic". The spitting is symbolic of Jadine's rejection by her own people.

The second encounter happens when she is entrapped in the lime of the swamp and she frantically tries to get out of it. The natural forces of the swamp are shown by Morrison as female. These women are hanging down the trees and are symbolic of the grandmothers, mothers and sisters of the past:

> [Women] were delighted when they first saw her, thinking a runaway child had been restored to them. But upon looking closer they saw it differently. This girl was fighting to get away from them.[7]

Later she tries to cleanse herself of the tar of the swamp. The tar here symbolizes the blackness she tries to resist, along with the qualities that "built and hold things together".

Jadine's lack of connection with her race causes the end of her relationship with Son. She is deficient in a 'building' capability, so their relationship does not hold together. She is unable to understand the significance of her own heritage. Son rebukes her for advocating the white man and his culture:

> Go have his children.... Feed, love and care for white people's children. That's what you were born for; that's what you have waited for all your life. So have that white's man's baby, that's your job. You have been doing it for two hundred years, you can do it for two hundred more. There are no 'mixed' marriages.... People don't mix races; they abandon them or pick them.[8]

Jade abandons her race in favor of the white race. She doesn't have that quality of black women that Morrison finds in black women of roots, the quality of being both "the nest and the adventure" both or "the ship and the harbor" both.

Black women need to deeply nourish their connection to their community. Morrison had denounced rootlessness in *Sula* and by means of various episodes she has shown her disapproval for Jadine too. She says in an interview: "The tragedy of the situation was not that she was a Tar Baby, but that she wasn't. She couldn't know, she could not hold anything to herself."[9]

Morrison's Tar Women

As discussed earlier, black feminism is remarkable for two things. Firstly, it celebrates the 'womanhood' of black women. While white feminism's approach is of 'equity', that is equality between men and women, black feminism's approach is the emphasis on 'difference'. Secondly, black feminism is rooted in black history and heritage and the connection with the lost home, Africa. Toni Morrison feels strongly about this. She denounces African-American women who are alienated from their past and ignorant of their rich black tradition. Sula and Jadine, the protagonist of *Sula* and *Tar Baby* are lost because they are not anchored in their heritage.

If Morrison has disapproved of Jadine's lost ways in *Tar Baby*, she has also celebrated the black women who, like Pilate, are preservers of black culture. The 'woman in yellow' she portrays in the Parisian supermarket is one of those black women who are confident of their womanhood and proud of their blackness. The description of this black woman arrests attention:

> Under her long canary yellow dress Jadine knew there was too much hip, too much bust. The agency would laugh her out of the lobby, so why was she and everybody in the store transfixed? The height? The skin like tar against the canary yellow dress?... She looked up then and they saw something in her eyes so powerful it had burnt away the eyelashes.[10]

The grace, the power and the stature of the woman comes from her self-confidence, her belief in herself. She feels comfortable in her tar black skin and seems to have a conviction that she is beautiful. She is not embarrassed of herself in a Parisian supermarket. Her strength makes people see her. Because her culture is authentic so she makes Jadine feel 'inauthentic'. The woman then choses three eggs and holds the eggs aloft between earlobe and shoulder. 'Eggs' appear in Morrison's narrative to symbolize 'origin' and 'roots'. Here the three eggs in the hand of the woman hint at her knowledge of her culture and her affiliation to her origins. It is this knowledge that gives her the assurance to live confidently in a world where the rules are set by the whites.

Ondine works as a cook in the Street vacational home. She has the dual responsibility of looking after her own family and working. She is concerned about the education of Jadine. Her maternal instincts are highly developed—she even took care of Michael, Margaret and Valerian's son, like her own child when he was a little boy. This is more than Margaret, his own mother did. Ondine's relationship with Sydney is a harmonious one. The value of love and stability comes from a 'tar'-like quality that Morrison claims black women possess. Ondine seeks fulfillment within the boundaries of her community. She tells Jadine what the role of a woman should be:

> ...a girl has got to be a daughter first. She have to learn that...I mean a real woman: a woman good enough for a child; good enough for a man—good enough even for the respect of other women.... A daughter is a woman that cares about where she come from and take care of them who took care of her.[11]

Like the 'woman in yellow' it is not physical beauty but sincerity and belief in her people that she needs to have.

Therese, who one used to serve in the house of Valerian Street, first seems to possess only minor importance in the novel but her significance increases as the novel progresses. Therese is the preserver of racial memory and practitioner of Voodoo. "She, physically [blind], like Tiresias, whom her name also suggests, truly sees".[12] She is blind but her blindness is magical. She has the ability to see the unseen and what people with eyes cannot see. She senses the presence of Son in Isle de Chevaliers and she names him chocolate eater. She acts as a mother to Son and supplies him with chocolate while he is hidden in the Street's house. She argues with Son to give up his search for Jadine saying that "Forget her.... She has forgotten her ancient properties."[13] Therese is the ancestor figure who guides Son in escaping from a superficial black girl back to his history and people. So she is one of Morrison's conjure women who "live always on the edge of both black and white cultures, relegated and sometimes confined to the wild zone, their magical powers contained but never completely dissipated."[14] We read that Therese's magic breasts continue giving milk forever. Milk of a mother is symbolic of life and one's origin like that of 'egg'. So, Therese becomes a symbol of a life-sustaining mother who knows how to take care of and nourish her child with ancient knowledge but "like the river deformed into a swamp, Therese has atrophied, her maternal function displaced by Enfamil formula."[15] But her image of nurturance never diminishes. Like Ondine she knows the importance of the connection with roots.

Ondine, the 'woman in yellow', and Therese are the principal women of the novel who are portrayed as authentic black women by Morrison. While Jadine is only the 'adventure' not the 'nest' these women are both. They are real 'tar women' who are approved by Morrison and who are capable of bringing progress to their community.

Black and White Difference

Toni Morrison never becomes oblivious of the difference between the lives of black and white people. In *Tar Baby*, she has juxtaposed black and white characters for the first time in her novels to study this difference.

Ondine is the industrious cook and housekeeper of Valerian's luxurious house. She shows a commitment to the Street family. She is also appreciated by the family but it is the same kind of appreciation that Pauline gets in the Fisher's house in *The Bluest Eye* and Corinthians in Michael Mary Graham's house in *Song of Solomon*. The bedroom of Margaret is 'sculptured' and lavish as is the mansion in which she lives. On the other hand, Morrison contrasts the room in which Sydney and Ondine live.

The difference between this room and rest of the house was marked. Here were second hand furniture, table scarves, tiny pillows, scatter rugs and the smell of human beings.... No visitors ever came in here. There were no extra chairs; no display of teaset. Just the things they used.[16]

Son finds this room very grand because he feels the smell of his people in it. Yet the difference between a black woman's room and a white woman's room is stark and drives home the point that there is vast disparity between the classes.

Another episode in the novel highlights the indifference of the white couple towards their black employees. The Street family does not even know the names of Gideon and Therese, though they have worked for them for many years. They call them Yardman and Mary following the pattern of white masters.

Valerian fires Gideon and Therese for stealing apples. At this point Son comments that though blacks are a major cause of the prosperity of whites in the Unites States, yet the whites are not ready to acknowledge this truth. He says:

> ...he had been able to dismiss with a flutter of the fingers the people whose sugar and cocoa had allowed him to grow in regal comfort; although he had taken the sugar and cocoa and paid for it as though it had no value, as though the cutting of cane and picking of beans was child's play and had no value....[17]

Tar Baby is a novel that works at multiple levels on important contemporary themes in black feminism. The novel stresses the significance of black culture and history for black women. Without this knowledge the progress of black women would be superficial. It affirms Toni Morrison as a black feminist who is concerned about her whole race rather than only its women. In the words of John Irving: "Morrison's greatest accomplishment is that she has raised her novel above the social realism that too many black novels and women's novels are trapped in. She has succeeded in writing about race and women symbolically."[18]

NOTES

1. Thomas LeClair. "'The Language must not Sweat': A Conversation with Toni Morrison." *Toni Morrison: Critical Perspectives—Past and Present*. Henry Louis Gates Jr. and K.A. Appiah (eds.) (New York: Amistad), 1993, p. 372.
2. Nellie McKay. *Critical Essays on Toni Morrison* (Boston, MA: GK Hall and Company), 1998, p. 175.
3. Barbara Hill Rigney. *The Voices of Toni Morrison* (Columbus: Ohio State University Press), 1991, p. 59.
4. Qtd. by Marilyn Sanders Mobley in "Narrative Dilemma: Jadine as Cultural Orphan in *Tar Baby*". *Toni Morrison: Critical Perspectives—Past and Present*. Henry Louis Gates, Jr. and K.A. Appiah (New York: Amistad), 1993, p. 288.
5. Toni Morrison. *Tar Baby* (London: Vintage), 1981, p. 72.
6. *Ibid*., p. 43.

7. *Ibid.*, p. 184.
8. *Ibid.*, p. 272.
9. Charles Ruass. *Conversations with American Writers* (New York: Alfred A. Knopf), 1984, p. 226.
10. Toni Morrison. *Tar Baby* (London: Vintage), 1981, p. 42.
11. *Ibid.*, p. 283.
12. Dorothy H. Lee. "The Quest for Self: Triumph and Failure in the Works of Toni Morrison". *Black Women Novelists 1950-1980: A Critical Evaluation.* Mary Ann Evans (Westport, CT: Greenwood Press), 2003, p. 357.
13. Toni Morrison. *Tar Baby* (London: Vintage), 1981, p. 308.
14. Barbara Hill Rigney. *The Voices of Toni Morrison* (Columbus: Ohio State University Press), 1991, p. 67.
15. Peter B. Erickson. "Images of Nurturance in *Tar Baby*" *Toni Morrison: Critical Perspectives—Past and Present.* Henry Louis Gates Jr. and K.A. Appiah (eds.) (New York: Amistad), 1993, p. 303.
16. *Ibid.*, p. 61.
17. Toni Morrison. *Tar Baby* (London: Vintage), 1981, p. 204.
18. John Irving. *New York Times Book Review*, March 29, 1981.

WORKS CITED

Evans, Mary Ann. *Black Women Novelists 1959-1980: A Critical Evaluation.* Westport, CT: Greenwood Press, 2003.

Hooks, Bell. *Feminist Theory: From Margin to Center.* Boston, MA: South End Pres, 1984.

Irving, John. *New York Times Book Review.* March 29, 1981.

Louis Gates Jr. Henry and K.A. Appiah (eds.) *Toni Morrison: Critical Perspectives—Past and Present.* New York: Amistad, 1993.

McKay, Nellie. *Critical Essays on Toni Morrison.* Boston: G.K. Hall and Company, 1998.

Morrison, Toni. *Tar Baby.* London: Vintage, 1981.

Rigney, Barbara Hill. *The Voices of Toni Morrison.* Columbus: Ohio State University Press, 1991.

Ruass, Charles. *Conversation with American Writers.* New York: Alfred A. Knopf, 1984.

Smith, Valerie. *Self-Discovery and Authority in African American Narrative.* Cambridge: Harvard University Press, 1987.

Susan, Ratcliffe (ed.). *Oxford Quotation and Proverbs.* New York: Oxford University Press.

5

Predicting the Future of Youngers in Clybourne Park: A Speculative Study of Lorraine Hansberry's *A Raisin in the Sun*

Shaharyar Haider

ABSTRACT

This paper presents an in-depth analysis of Hansberry's *A Raisin in the Sun* as a text about Afro-American quest for identity and the dreams about equality. The class between white and Afro-American communities is highlighted as the main hindrance for a coexistent society. Moreover, it sheds light on the Afro-American characters' struggle for connecting themselves to their identity, and roots. Asagai, a character in Hansberry's text, is a metaphorical representation of the anti-assimilative Afro-Americans. It further analyses the decision of Youngers, an Afro-American family in Hansberry's text, of moving to Clybourne Park. It invokes apocalyptic fears because the white community won't be welcoming them. It concludes with the socio-economic challenge that the marginalized family would face in the new community.

Keywords: Assimilative, Apocalyptic, Marginalized.

The future of Youngers, an African-American family, is at stake when they leave for a white community, Clybourne Park. Their survival is in question as black people aren't welcomed there. There are several questions about Youngers', an Afro-American family in *A Raisin in the Sun,* living in Clybourne Park. The first thing for them will be their survival. It would not be easy for them to fit in a white community. The resistance of white people will be a torture for them. The most problematic thing for them would be the social rejection. They will be treated as outcasts and nobody will befriend them. Another problem is the economic status. In a community where Afro-Americans are taken as threats, it would be difficult for them to find economic prosperity.

Beneatha is an intellectual character who needs peace of mind to ponder over the issues of identity, race and culture. It would be impossible for her to find equality there, which she had so long been thinking of. He quest for the search of her identity can bring more frustration to her while living in a white community. She rejects the proposal of Harrison who tries to be like the white Americans. It would not be easy for her to live in a community where she will be antagonized by the white neighbors.

In the play *A Raisin in the Sun*, Youngers make repeated endeavors to get out of the poverty line. Youngers leave for Clybourne Park, an area where white people live. They have threats and fears about being tortured or irritated there but they show a will to go there. The two dreams that the Youngers family want to fulfil are to be accepted by the white society and to be financially stable. Every character has their own dream and they make efforts for achieving it. The conflict arises when we see the clash of the dreams of two characters. Walter is fed up of his job of a limousine driver. Ruth seems to be content with their lot but Walter is not, he desperately wishes to become wealthy.

The robustness of the "American Dream" has made material prosperity the truth of all times. The thing that never varies about the American Dream is that everyone pursues something in life. People make endeavors to materialize their dreams. Some are beaten by the cruel reality of the American Economic System while others taste success. Everyone in America wants to have some kind of financial success in his or her life. The "American

Dream" means that each man has the right to go for the pursuit of happiness and strive for the best.

He plans to invest in a liquor store in partnership with Willy Harris, a street-smart acquaintance of Walter whom we never see. Beneatha wants to become a doctor and Mama is ready to provide tuition. Mama's own dream is to buy a house of their own. The tension emerges from Walter's effort to be in liquor business. Mama has religious objections to alcohol so she remains resilient in giving money to Walter for it. Walter remains whining because nobody bothers about his dream.

At times it seems to us that it is simply is not possible for everyone to become prosperous through determination and hard work. The consequences of this belief can include the poor feeling that it is their fault that they are not successful. It can also result in less effort towards helping the poor since their poverty is "proof" of their laziness. It then, consciously or inadvertently, divides society into haves and have-nots. The notion of the "American Dream" also ignores other factors of success such as the family and wealth one is born into and inheritable traits such as intelligence.

The Youngers' dream is to get their own house and move into a better area. They also want to be accepted by the white society and to become financially stable. Their individual dreams prove that they think about change in their position. Beneatha who is Walter's sister wants to go to school to become a doctor, but in those times people of color weren't considered for high positions. Walter, on the other hand, wants to own his own business, which was a liquor store, but Mama doesn't want to spend her money on that.

In a high tension scene, Walter presents severe critique, specifically, of the role of Ruth and generally, the women in making men's destinies. He blames Ruth for not encouraging him. He objects her statement "eat your eggs" as an escapist attempt. His view of women is that they don't realize to the dreams of their men and remain contented with whatever their lot is. Neither they take steps for change nor would they allow their men to do anything for the betterment of their situation.

His frustration speaks of the racial prejudice and economic problems of American society. Especially, it unravels the hatred for a black in a white society. Walter wants to prove his identity for which he wants Ruth to motivate him.

The poor black man does not exist in a cultural vacuum, but is rather an expressive of the cultural crossing, mixing, and engagement of black male culture with the values, attitudes, and concerns of the white majority. The reactionary behaviors and coping mechanisms that manifest from this cultural group may appear incomprehensible to one who is not challenged with an anomalous form of self-awareness defined by a conflicting identity that forces the black male to view himself through the lens of the dominant culture that does not perceive and does not allow him to function as equal. Hansberry's "foremost commitment, of course, was to the liberation of her fellow blacks in America, and here too she noted the human capacity of self-transcendence" (Carter 46).

Walter's urge to go into liquor business, which was prohibited at that time, shows his hasty invention of a short cut. He expresses his dissatisfaction with the job of a chauffeur. He ventures to go into an illegal business which marks his dissatisfied will. It shows the social structure of society where the black men have to struggle hard for finding out the true meaning of their lives. "Walter's dream remains only that not because of the defects in American system but because of basic flaws in his own character" (Washington 120).

Beneatha's defiant nature speaks of the revolutionary seeds in the youth of black Americans. She rejects the religious views of Mama and does not conform to Walter's urge for business. She presents a symbolic solution, education, for the problems of Afro-Americans. Her intellectual debates for equality and the importance of dreams are significant. Asagai, her university friend, is another ray of hope for the oppressed black Americans but he is soon rejected. The problem with his solution is that he offers an escapist window. He proposes Beneatha for marriage and wants her to go back to Nigeria. It seems to be an attempt of withdrawal from the 'battle front'. Beneatha does not give any clear response to him which shows her reluctance in giving up.

She turns down the proposal of Harrison as she does not like the black families who remain inclined to become like white. She declares rich black families worse than the white families. Her dislike for the hybrid families is a pronouncement of her pride in her own identity. Homi K. Bhabha has given the notion of hybridism in culture. We find the same thing in Harrison. He loves to be like white Americans and that is something which irritates Beneatha. Bhabha's "hybridization" describes the emergence of new cultural forms from multiculturalism. Hansberry has shown the diversity of American culture but not as a compliment. Her concern is to expose the hate for Afro-American people in white Americans.

Beneatha remains proud of her own culture, and she does not submit herself to the white American culture. Her intellectual debates with her university fellow, Asagai reflect the resistance in black people, their struggle to maintain their identity and instincts of survival in a culture where they are not accepted. Beneatha says to Mr. Asagai, "I want very much to talk with you. About Africa. You see, Mr. Asagai, I am looking for my identity!" (Hansberry 62). Her quest for her genesis is indirectly telling us about the awareness of black Americans about their roots. Her control of words and assertion of her will prove that she is determined to explore the new horizons.

Within the cultural framework of America, the systemic structure is characterized by white male patriarchy that allows for black people to have the ability to negotiate the way in which they have been socialized and institutionalized to think, act, and behave because they are men. However, the reality of race and the lack of diversity in the purest sense impede upon this effort and cripple the black people's ability to truly transition into maturity. They are left to constantly struggle and fight for an identity, for power, for respect, and for understanding who they are.

The pressure to conform to white male patriarchal standards of man as a protector, disciplinarian, and provider are representative of such a dilemma for black males. Despite the unconscious internalization and acceptance of the white male patriarchal standards, inequities in education and employment and limited access to educational opportunities that prevent the expression of these behaviors. This is the reason for which we do not see Travis getting the comforts, usually enjoyed by the kids.

The hopes of Younger family depend on the arrival of the insurance cheque. Walter wants it to be invested in liquor business, Beneatha needs it for her study and Mama wants to buy a house. When they receive the insurance check in the mail, Mama goes out and buys a house in the white neighborhood. Shortly after she buys the house, Clybourne Park authorities quickly send a representative by the name of Karl Lindner. Lindner is a part of the New Neighbors Orientation Committee that welcomes newcomers in the neighborhood. Linder asks them to sell their house as they would not be able to fit themselves in the new area. Moreover, the people of Clybourne Park won't welcome them. It involves irony as the member of welcome committee is asking the would-be newcomers not to move in that area. Lindner states, "It is a matter of the people of Clybourne Park believing, rightly or wrongly, as I say, that for the happiness of all concerned that our Negro families are happier when they live in their own communities" (Hansberry 118).

This basically states that the Youngers don't fit into the description of that community. This is an example of them not being accepted by the white society. Being financially stable allows people to have a better lifestyle, earn respect from others and obtain power. People can live better because they don't have to worry about their basic needs. They never bother about the payment of bills as it's a minor issue for them. They don't need to dream of their own business as they already have it.

Somehow, Walter takes 6500$ from Mama which would be divided between him and Beneatha. His hasty urge of achieving his dream tempts him to give all that money to Willy Harris for getting the liquor store started but the friend takes the money and flees with it. Money would allow a person to gain respect. Being financially able, we never let people look down upon us. Poor Afro-American Walter gets deceived by his own friend, who adds insult to his injuries. The American people view the "American Dream" as a dream of a land in which life should be better and richer and fuller for everyone, with opportunity for each according to ability or achievement. But it does not happen with Walter; he does not show his ability to achieve his dream and eventually gets rated as a failure.

The pressure to conform to white male patriarchal standards of manhood as protector, disciplinarian, and provider are representative of such a dilemma for black males. Despite the unconscious internalization and acceptance of the white male patriarchal standards, inequities in education and employment and limited access to educational opportunities prevent the expression of these behaviors. This is the reason for which we do not see Travis getting the comforts, usually enjoyed by the kids.

Mama is the nucleus of family. She has a firm control of family matters. She asserts her authority and keeps her family united. When Walter tries to assert his will, Mama reminds him "Ain't nobody said you wasn't grown. But you still in my house and my presence" (Hansberry 71). She has a dream of house which she materializes. She pacifies Ruth when she gets worried about going into Clybourne Park. Ruth says, "Mama, there ain't no colored people living in Clybourne Park" (Hansberry 93). Mama simply replies, "Well, I guess there's going to be some now" (Hansberry 93).

Karl Lindner, the representative of the Clybourne Park Improvement Association comes to see Youngers. He tries to convince them not to move in the white community. He creates an aura of fear and threat that the community will not welcome them. He urges them to sell the house to the community. He acts as the personification of white strata of society which is unwilling to incorporate the blacks within it. He says, "Our association is prepared, through the collective effort of our people, to buy the house from you at a financial gain to your family" (Hansberry 118).

Walter sends Lindner back by saying that they don't want to give up the idea of going to the white community. He and

Beneatha enjoy that ecstatic moment in which they turn out a white man. They get an air of superiority because Walter foresees the money coming from liquor business. His expectation of short-cut richness makes him oblivious of reality. He, for the time being, goes to the realm of imagination and starts singing:

> I got wings...you got wings.
>
> All God's children got wings.... (Hansberry 122)

Walter is brought back to the real world, when Bobo comes with news about Willy. His haunted frightened eyes convey an ominous sense. He tells to Walter that Willy has deceived them and he has run away with Walter's money. It strikes Walter like a bolt from the blue and he starts cursing Willy. His expectations are hurt and the short cut brings failure to his destiny. Out of desperation he whines, "That money is made out of my father's flesh" (Hansberry 128). For him, all is gone but there is a hope of going to Clybourne Park to find his new identity. Wilkerson has written, "Walter Lee, reaching a new level of maturity and the family moving into a new home, emphasizes the triumph of this working-class Black family" (646).

There comes another question about the future of Travis. In his age, children usually are in the process of making their identity. He is a child who will be more submissive to the environment of Clybourne Park. The white folks around him can cause an inferiority complex in him. It is also notable that will he be able to assert his own identity by being proud of it or he will find an erosion of self-esteem there? Moreover, it would be very difficult for him to understand the color difference, and realize that 'black is beauty'. The future of the baby in Ruth's womb is also under scrutiny here. It would be difficult for him to bridge the gap between his home and the white community outside. He can go for the trends of being white or having a likeness for white people.

In this environment of uncertainty, Mama's plant is the ray of hope. It symbolizes her faith in her roots, African identity and the meaning of her creed. She dreams of a community in Clybourne Park where they would equally live with the white Americans. "She has always striven to attain a higher existence in this world" (Nemiroff 27). Youngers vow not to create any problem for their new neighbors. They hope for a peaceful life in the new community where they will find the essence of their creed and they will be able to carve out a stone of hope from the mountain of despair. It can be said that they will be able to "hold these truths to be self-evident that all men are created equal".

WORKS CITED

Carter, Steven R. (Autumn, 1980) *Commitment Amid Complexity: Lorraine Hansberry's Life in Action:* Oxford University Press, Vol. 7. (No. 3). Retrieved from Jstor http://www.jstor.org/stable/467027

Hansberry, Lorraine. *A Raisin in the Sun*. New York: Vintage Books, 1994.

Nemiroff, Robert. (Spring 1988) *A Raisin in the Sun: After 25 Years More Significant Than Ever:* University of Illinois Press, Vol. 3 (No 2). Retrieved from Jstor http://www.jstor.org/stable/40545519

Shannon, Sandra G. (Winter, 1991) *From Lorraine Hansberry to August Wilson: An Interview With Lloyd Richards:* The Johns Hopkins University Press, Vol. 14 (No. 1). Retrieved from Jstor http://www.jstor.org/stable/2931445

Washington, J. Charles. (Spring 1988) "*A Raisin in the Sun* Revisited." *Black American Literature Forum*, Vol. 22 (No. 1). Retrieved from Jstor http://www.jstor.org/stable/2904153

Wilkerson, Margaret B. (Dec., 1986) *"A Raisin in the Sun": Anniversary of an American Classic:* The Johns Hopkins University Press, Vol. 38 (No. 4). Retrieved from Jstor http://www.jstor.org/stable/3208286

Wilkerson, Margaret B. (Winter, 1987) *The Dark Vision of Lorraine Hansberry: Excerpts from a Literary Biography:* The Massachusetts Review, Inc., Vol. 28 (No. 4). Retrieved from Jstor http://www.jstor.org/stable/25089915

6

The Expression of Human Predicament in the Poetry of Robert Frost

Neena Sharma

ABSTRACT

Robert Frost is considered a great American poet chiefly because he has presented the scene of human dilemma. During his eighty-eight years, Robert Frost became the most read and honored American poet of the twentieth century. During his long poetic career, Robert Frost composed poems and published them in the form of several volumes. Robert Frost's poetry can definitely be called the poetry of human beings. He reveals himself through his poems as a student of nature. His poems reveal the expression of human predicament. A human being in the grip of alienation, despair and disillusionment. Frost's people suffer in the hands of nature. They have their personal problems. A human being in the poems of Robert Frost has to face unpleasant situations. His first volume of poems shows the maturity of Robert Frost's powers about the expression of human predicament. It expresses the tone of disappointment. In 'North of Boston', he tells the story of conflict. His third volume contains a wider variety of poems and deals with human difficulties. This volume represents Robert Frost's reflective mood. The poem "In the Home Stretch" is a story of a couple, moving in to an isolated farm. This paper focuses on the aspect that loneliness and fear of loneliness are always present in the human heart. Man is alone, aliented and his alienation becomes the source of human predicament.

Keywords: Predicament, Loneliness, Unpleasant, Reflective, Conflict, Alienation.

Just as Thomas Hardy was the novelist of human predicament, Robert Frost is the poet of the human predicament also. The truth is that all good literature is an exercise of the artist to place before the world the sorry state of this world which is really not habitable but which, most helplessly, we have to face. Man is alone even amidst the crowd. The tragedy is that he is never properly understood. The greatest irony is that those who claim to have understood him have actually misunderstood him. Since the poet is a sensitive creature, he is capable of looking deep into the things. He knows that there is great difference between the resemblance and the actual state but his problem is to exist and survive. He has to make adjustments with the forces quite contrary to his nature.

Robert Frost is considered a great American poet chiefly because he has presented the scene of human dilemma. During his eighty-eight years, Robert Frost became the most read and honored American poet of the twentieth century. During his long poetic career Robert Frost composed poems and published them in the form of several volumes. These volumes are entitled. *A Boy's Will*, *North of Boston*, *Mountain Interval*, *New Hampshire*, *West Running Brook* and *A Further Range*. He also wrote two dramas *A Masque of Reason* and *A Masque of Mercy*.

Robert Frost's poetry can definitely be called the poetry of human beings. He reveals himself through his poems as a student of nature. His poems reveal the expression of human predicament. A human being in the grip of alienation, despair and disillusionment. Frost's people suffer in the hands of nature. They have their personal problems. A human being in the poems of Robert Frost has to face unpleasant situations. Robert Frost has offered a good many definitions of poetry. One of them shows the expression of predicament.

Every poem is an epitome of the great
predicament; a figure of the will braving
alien entanglements.

Robert Frost's first volume of verses was published in London in 1913 and was entitled *A Boy's Will*. It shows the maturity of Robert Frost's powers about the expression of human predicament. It expresses the tone of disappointment. This volume represents the voice of Robert Frost through the medium of ordinary human being. *A Boy's Will* takes its title from Longfellow's *My Lost Youth*, *A Boy's Will* is the wind's will; it echoes Shakespeare, John Keats, P.B. Shelley and Tennyson in vocabulary and diction.

A Boy's Will consisted of thirty-two poems divided into three parts. Part first begins with the theme of withdrawal from the world and ends on a note of one kind of return to it. Part second represents some areas of experience and part third represents the acceptance of a person's confrontation with life. *A Boy's Will* depicts the various stages of a young man's outlook in life. It contains a number of poems that are counted among Robert Frost's best poems including "My November Guest". "Love and a Question", "The Vantage Point", "Reluctance" and "Mowing". They all deal with human predicament. "My November Guest" is the third poem of this volume. The guest is sorrow. Sorrow is personified in this poem. "My November Guest" gives the expression to the poet's love of bare November days, before the coming of snow. The poet talks about desolation, deserted trees and the faded earth. The poem is remarkable for its mixture of joy and sorrow. The paradox of joy in the scene of desolation is note worthy.

She is glad the birds are gone away,
She's glad her simple worsted gray
Is silver now with clinging mist.

Loneliness and fear of loneliness are always present in the human heart. Man is alone, aliented and his alienation becomes the source of human predicament. "Reluctance" is another poem of Robert Frost. He mainly dealt with nature but man is rarely absent. He is always present is his nature poems. He introduces a keen human emotion into a nature poem.

Robert Frost deals with a lot of common men who suffer from unpleasant situations on this earth. Human destiny is confronted with a hostile universe. Robert Frost presents man in a state of alienation. Frost treats man as an integral part of the universe, but there are difficulties which a human being has to face in his life. Robert Frost's volume *A Boy's Will* presents the ordinary joys and sorrows of man's life.

His best poem "Love and a Question" is totally an expression of human predicament. The reader is left to guess what actually happens in this poem. A man and his young wife are disturbed suddenly. They face an unpleasant situation on their marriage eve. They are unable to think, what they should do in this situation. The situation is that a stranger asks for a shelter for the night. The situation is unusal for them because it is their marriage eve. The bride groom has been waiting to spend time with his bride, but there is obstacle between them.

It is the expression of human predicament whether should keep the stranger in the bridal house or should he say 'no' and send the stranger back. The bride, is inside the room, waiting for her husband.

> Within, the bride in the dusk alone
> bent over the open fire,
> Her face rose-red with the glowing coal
> And the thought of her heart's desire.

This poem shows a clear picture of human predicament in the life of the bride and bride groom.

"The Trial by Existence", when it appeared in *A Boy's Will* would be the longest poem in this volume. It gives a point that death is not the end of life but the beginning of another life. It reflects the circle of life. In another life, the same struggle will go on. Man will have to face difficulties. After serving in the last struggle, man is transported to a paradise. Newly assembled souls are gathered together and instructed by God for a trial. In writing "The Trial by Existence", Robert Frost tried to build up some of the attitudes and recommendations he had met in

James's "Will to Believe" essay. Robert Frost said about *A Boy's Will*—

> An expression of my life for the ten
> years from eighteen on when I thought I
> greatly preferred stocks and stone to people.

This remark would refer to the years 1892-1901. These were his years of different employments, his courtship and marriage with Elionor white, ending more or less with the death of his mother and his first child. Robert Frost had to face sufferings in his life. "The Trial by Existence" insists that the essence of life is to choose correctly and then to get 'what we some how chose'. Robert Frost had written a letter to Sussan Hayes Ward in May 1913 with reference to poems from his first volume *A Boy's Will.*

> *A Boy's Will* itself, it is worth a moment's
> pause to ask how those poems are "the
> expression of a life was forced to live".

Robert Frost's another poem, "Reluctance" is a description of human complexities of desire and responsibility. The natural scene reveals a keen human emotion in this poem. "My Butterfly" was composed due to the most disturbing episode in Robert Frost's courtship. It deals with human predicament in the life of an ordinary human being. Other poems in this volume include "Star", "The Vantage Point", "Mowing", "Revelation", "The Tuft of Flowers", "The Demiurge's Laugh".

In all the poems of *A Boy's Will*, it would be too simple to see a human being as a sentimental victim of circumstances. Human being is forced by domestic situations and social difficulties. They all deal with human difficulties.

Robert Frost's second volume *North of Boston* (1914) was published by David Nutt; London. It tells the story of conflict. In *North of Boston*, he has presented the most bleak picture and depressing view of life. The poems "Home Burial", "The Fear", "The Death of the Hired Man" deal with alienation. The poems he was writing for *North of Boston* have subjects like the death of an old man or the presence of the dead child in the mind of living parents as in "Home Burial". He used *North of*

Boston subtitled *The Book of People*. The subtitle is crucial and quite popular. Robert Frost wrote to Sidney Cox about *North of Boston*—

> No Book of verse has had as much space given it for a good while.

Robert Frost presents a picture in "Home Burial", of what happens when a human being cannot accept the fact of his conditions. The young wife in this poem is unable to reconcile with the death of her child. Robert Frost took the story from his personal experience. His sister Jeanie was unable to face the coarseness and brutality of existence. Jeanie's ideal word could never be reconciled with the actual word. She became alienated from the world. In this poem, there is a conflict between real facts of life and the imagined view of a young wife. The people in *North of Boston* are depicted in their conflict with the problem of existence in this world.

> You could sit there with the stains on your shoes
> of the fresh earth from whom your own baby's grave
> And talk about your every day concerns
> I can repeat the very words you were saying.

"The Black Cottage" is a story about an old lady whose husband served in Union Army. Her son left her alone after the death of the father. It is a bitter truth of life that parents teach their children every thing about evil and good. They think that their children will look after their parents in the old age. But it is life's reality that at the time of old age, they leave their parents in loneliness. In "The Black Cottage", Robert Frost has repeated the same bitter truth and life's reality. He imagines himself to be 'Monarch of a desert land'.

Robert Frost declared to Louis Untermeyer soon after *North of Boston* was published—

> it begins as a lump in a throat, a sense
> wrong, a homesickness, a lovesickness. It is
> never a thought to begin with.... A poem
> particularly must not begin with thought first.

"A Servant to Servants" is the tale of the uncle. He went mad from intolerable disappointment in love. The poem involves the psychological self-revelation of a person. A farmer's wife is tired of cooking meals and housekeeping for the hired man. It seems to her that she is a servant to servants. The poet offers a shock when the mad man's niece discloses a sense of isolation. She reveals that she has once stayed in mental asylum and goes on to narrate the story of her mad uncle. It is a story of absolute horror. It is a story of conflict due to her loneliness, fear and purposelessness.

North of Boston portrays the darker aspects of life in New England. Robert Frost's interest in many of these poems is psychological. He was concerned with the motives and hidden nature of men and women, particularly of women. When Randall Jarell interviewed him at the Library of Congress in 1959, he said that he had tried to write poems for *North of Boston* without villains:

In tragic life no villain need be.

In the sense of tragic scenes he is not like William Shakespeare because Shakespeare could not write without villains in his dramas. No one is to blame as in "Home Burial" the husband is blamed by his wife on the death of their young children. Robert Frost's efforts was to attempt a truly represented life and conflict in the life of human being.

"A Hundred Collars" dramatizes a familiar human conflict. It deals with the fear of unfamiliar. A timid professor is forced to share a room with a stranger in a one hotel town. It seems to the professor that the other person may be a murderer and a robber. His nervousness makes clear to stranger that the professor is fearful due to his presence in a room. He is broad-minded and tries to ignore his insult. He reassures the professor that he himself had more money than him. The stranger is angry to learn that the fear is motivated by thorough mistrust. After all, he has ninety dollars in his own wallet compared to professor's five dollars. Now who has the right to suspicion? He advises the professor—

> You'd better tuck your money under you
> And sleep on it the way I always do
> When I am with people I don't trust at Night.

Later, he unpacks his whisky bottle and goes out. He leaves the professor quaking on his pillow. The professor's condition is the expression of human predicament in which he was unable to think, what to do in this unpleasant situation especially, when he had to share his room with a stranger whom he was thinking to be a robber and murderer.

At least one critic, Louise Bogan, agreed and in her brief survey of American poetry, she took a similar line by saying that Robert Frost in *North of Boston*—

> Briefly possessed himself of a human realism and insight which
> he was never quite able to repeat.

Robert Frost has presented the terrible actualities of life in a new way. The poem like "Mending Wall" puts up a question Do men work together or apart? Robert Frost says that they do both. But in reality they stand so far apart from each other that even the simplest communication proves futile. Miss Lowell declares that—

> *North of Boston* is a very sad book...which
> in spite of its author's sympathetic touch....
> reveals a disease that is eating in to the vitals
> of our New England life, at least in its rural communities.

Another poem, "After Apple-Picking" is a dramatic monologue of an exhausted apple-picker. The scent of apple makes him lazy so that the world looks strange to him. It embodies a universal experience and conflict in the mind of the speaker about the task of apple-picking. In another poem, "The Fear" he shows the feeling of guilt in a young woman who has left one man and has been living with her lover on a lonely farm. She always lives with the feeling of guilt. Robert Frost represents it as a story of conflict in a woman and her fear from society.

Robert Frost's other poems from this volume are also the expression of human predicament. It includes such poems as, "The Code", "The Mountain", "Blueberries", "The Housekeeper" and "The Wood pile", etc.

Robert Frost's third volume of poems *Mountain Interval* was published is 1916. This volume contains a wider variety of poems and deals with human difficulties. The interval in the title means lower land between hills, usually with some kind of stream. Robert Frost made clear that he was using the word 'interval' for its double meaning to recall elinor as a dedication. The volume had particular significance for Elinor, as well as Robert Frost, for a good reason. "It contains thirty-two poems. Twenty-four of the thirty-two poems were written on one of Frost's farms. Eleven were written from Derry. Thirteen came from Bethlehem and Franconia".

This volume represents Robert Frost's reflective mood. The poem "In the Home Stretch" is a story of a couple, moving to an isolated farm. It was derived directly from Robert Frost and Elinor's experience. The book *Mountain Interval* includes both rhymed lyrics and dramatic narrative in blank verse, along with a ballad and three poems for children. Robert Frost's characteristic theme of isolation, loneliness and fear are expressed in "An Old Man's Winter Night" and "The Hill Wife" which must have reminded him of how hard and lovely his years as a New England farmer had been.

In his great poem "An Old Man's Winter Night", Robert Frost explains that the human insecurity is clear. He emphasizes upon man's alienation continually. It shows the condition of man in an empty universe. The poem is both a reflection on the state of being old and a lender. It reveals the portrait of a particular character. Robert Frost represents an old man who is alone in the farm house on a winter night. The poet describes his sleep as a living death in which physical organs continue to function. The poem is a definition of death itself.

> One aged man—one man—can't keep a house
> A farm, a countary side, or if he can,
> it's thus he does it of a winter night.

Thus, all the volumes, *A Boy's Will*, *North of Boston*, *Mountain Intervel*, *New Hampshire*, *A Further Range* are the expression of human problems which he has to face in his life.

WORKS CITED

Bogan, Louise. *Achievement in American Poetry*. Chicago: Henry Regenry, 1951.

Frost, Robert. *The Years of Triumph*. New York: Holt, Rinehart and Winston, 1970.

Lathem, Edward C. "My November Guest". *The Poetry of Robert Frost*. New York: Holt, Rinehart and Winston, 1969.

Pritchard, William H. *Frost: A Literary Life Reconsidered*. New York: OUP, 1984.

Thompson, Lawrence. *Selected Letters of Robert Frost*. New York: Holt, Rinehart and Winston, 1964.

7

Conflicts and Adjustments in Marital Life: A Study of Neil Simon's *Jake's Women*

P. Padma

ABSTRACT

The most formidable comedy writer in American Theatre of the contemporary times, the darling of mass audience, Neil Simon is the favorite whipping boy for cultural mandarins. Apart from William Shakespeare's plays, it is only Simon's plays that ran four at a time in Broadway Theatre. Born in 1927, in a poor Jewish family, Marvin Neil Simon has become the most commercially successful playwright in the history of the American Theatre. Speaking about Simon, David Richards explained in *Washington Post*, "Simon's comedies have run forever on Broadway and made him pots of money, after which they were turned into movies that made him pots more".[1] Apart from writing scripts for television and radio, he has to his credit more than thirty-six plays, screen plays and a two volume auto-biography. Before Simon has set a trend, the Broadway theatre for a very long time was popular for performing tragedies written by Eugene O'Neill, Arthur Miller and Tennessee Williams. In spite of winning many awards, critics have not placed Simon in his due position partly because he has written to masses and partly because of the genre he has chosen. Comedy, though was born at the same time as tragedy, it was never given the same position right from the times of Aristotle. Though critics dismissed Simon's plays as light hearted entertainment, he captivated audience for more than five decades and he enjoyed popularity in his own time. The present paper is focused on *Jake's Wife*.

Keywords: Marital life, Conflicts, Marriages, Adjustments, Expressionistic Play.

Conflicts in marital life and the adjustments one has to make to save one's family life are projected in Neil Simon's romantic comedies, *Bare Foot in the Park* (1963) and *Chapter Two* (1977) which are based on the early married life of Simon with Joan, his first wife and when he married again after her death respectively. *Jake's Women* (1992) is also an auto-biographical play. Unfortunately, God had not decided one marriage for Simon and when he gets married for the second time, he took some time to adjust and this is projected in *Chapter Two* but why things could not work out well in spite of his 'golden mean' is projected in the next play *Jake's Women*. In fact, writing has helped him to overcome problems in married life to a certain extent. He married five times in his life. After the death of his first wife Joan, he married Marsha Mason, next Diane Lander and lastly some young lady Elaine Joyce.

Paul and Corie Batter in a *Bare Foot in the Park* are a newly-married couple experiencing certain internal and external obstacles in the first week of their marriage before restoring it to harmony. This is a light-hearted comedy in which the Batters learn the value of moderation and compromise which he called "the golden mean".

When Neil Simon published *Chapter Two* in 1977, the number of divorces and second marriages had drastically increased in United States and loneliness was the biggest problem in America. Simon has objectified in this drama his subjective pain at the loss of his beloved wife, Joan and the problems surrounding his marriage, several months later to his second wife, actress Marsha Mason. Leo and Faye, the second pair is in contrast to them being unfaithful to their partners and they involve in extra-marital affairs and the sense of guilt spoils Leo's sense of happiness. Simon sounds didactic in bringing out the futility of such infidelity. The play is also self-reflexive because the protagonist comments on the craft of writing for commercial success and for the satisfaction of being a writer. 'A Golden Mean' to the Odd Couple which Simon suggests in these plays is projected even in his next play *Jake's Women.*

In *Jake's Women*, Simon brings in different women related to Jake. He projects his love for his mother and his relationship with first wife which come in his way to understand his second wife in proper light. His daughters and sister also figure in his imaginative conversation and contribute to understand himself first and later to understand his second wife to bridge their relationship. In fact, the second and third plays play a significant role to analyze his conduct to adjust in his married life.

Running parallel to it is his profession as a writer which also plays a major role in bringing conflicts that arose between him and his second wife. The play is filled with imaginative conversations with all the women in his life and hence it takes place both, in his office room in his house and in his mind as flash backs. Occasionally, he is interrupted by phone calls and by the arrival of his wife, Maggie. The introspections help him to understand his wife and analyze the situations better to resolve his conflicts with his wife and to make adjustments to bring a happy end to their married life. Thus, the intermingling of his profession and married life is clearly projected in Simon's *Jake's Women.*

Simon wrote *Jake's Women* in 1992 and opened it in San Diego, but he revised it before presenting it in Broadway theatre. In this play, he experiments adopting expressionistic technique to reveal what goes on in the mind of the middle-aged protagonist, Jake, a writer like Simon himself. The influence of Arthur Miller's *Death of a Salesman* is clearly visible when he uses the technique to reveal what goes on 'inside the mind' of Jake. Consumed by his work he becomes emotionally isolated from the life he leads. He participates less and observes more. The play is filled with imaginative conversations and flash backs. Simon partly projects on different women in his life—his deceased wife, second wife, his daughters, sister and so on. The protagonist's search for human connection is projected in *Jake's Women*.

Departing from his usual realistic technique, much of the drama is inside the mind of the protagonist, therefore, it moves between the present and the past; between the fact and fantasy. The setting is both the apartment in which he lives and his mind. The usage of apartment is minimal which is evident in the following lines:

> The apartment is minimal, his mind is over flowing. There are no walls, no windows; no sense of place and even time is indefinite.[2]

The apartment is sparingly furnished with a chair, table and word-processor.

The people whom he imagines "seemingly appear from nowhere and leave in the same way".[3] They are mostly the women who have played a significant role in his life as his first wife, Julie, who dies in an automobile accident some ten years ago. Occasionally, he is interrupted by some events that happen in his real life as a phone call or the arrival of his wife, Maggie. As critic Jack Kroll observes, Simon mixes "time periods and states of mind in an often brilliant cross fire of confrontations".[4] Like Eugene Jerome in the play *Brighton Beach* trilogy, Jake here breaks through the imaginary fourth wall and speaks to the audience, he introduces the characters and comments on their actions and is humorous some times in the delivery of dialogues. For example, he explains that his sister, Karen has attended a film school in New York University and "made a three-hour student film of her, just sitting on a kitchen chair, called 'Loneliness'" (*JW* 163).

Jake at times speaks to the audience to reveal his innermost thoughts and again it is different from a soliloquy, in that the protagonist does not involve in just revealing their psychology or inner most thoughts. Here Jake shares with the audience and make them part of their imaginary conversation. For example, Jake says, "we're all writers in a sense" (*JW* 163) and so they create imaginary scenes and conversations:

> There's not one of you who hasn't thought...of what it would be like to talk to your father who died five or twenty years ago. Would he look the same? Would you still be his little girl?... Or the boy you loved in college who married someone else. What would your life be if he proposed to you instead?... You've played that scene out. We all do it. (*JW* 218)

Jake is a writer and Maggie has her own business-career. They both are so absorbed in their work that they have developed relations also with the people with whom they work and prove unfaithful to each other and their eight years of marriage is in trouble. Jake feels that his dead wife is more dear to him and also his profession and that he is more connected with the characters he creates, while she is left behind and this makes her feel that she is "a rewrite of someone else" (*JW* 181).

Rather than facing his wife Maggie directly, he withdraws himself into the world of writing and constructs imaginative conversation with Maggie recalling the lovely days of their first meeting. He also creates characters as his sister Karen or his daughter, Molly as they are more sympathetic in understanding him and they comfort him. He also takes refugee entering into imaginary conversation with his first deceased wife, who understands his dependency. In the conversation, Julie says, "Now I see why you bring him back" (*JW* 185). She understands his weakness, "it's mostly when you are in trouble, isn't it? (*JW* 185).

The imaginative conversations have functional value in the play. They are not just used to comfort him. They give him chance to undergo retrospection and help him to analyze the situation better. In the process, he understands his own weakness and he is harsh at times punishing himself. His sister speaks to him harshly when he admits his infidelity to Maggie. He is able to understand why he is making her sister irritate him. Simon summons all women who are close to him and that he is the maker of his own destiny. She says, "You're unhappy if you want to be. You're lonely if you want to be. It's your choice" (*JW* 177).

Audience can easily recognize many problems in the play, may be the writer's own problems. Audience is pulled here into the mind of the writer to create. As Clive Barnes notices, "a bizarrely convincing portrait of the artist as a hall of mirrors".[5] Audience play the role of analyst as Brian Rhinehart observes:

> By making the audience an observer of Jake's psychic processes, Simon...open(s) up a kind of transferential dialogue between the individual audience member and the performance. It's not surprising that Simon enjoys the moniker 'Doc Simon'. He seems to know that people benefit from his art, just as an analyst benefits, through processes of transference, from a dialogue with a patients.[6]

Jake enjoys the sense of omnipotence that his writings provide him. His small room is his world and it appears as though he needs some control, but Jake is aware that he never has any control when reality begins. In Act II when Maggie separates from him for a period of six months, he loses his imaginative power also. Both his personal and professional life is in shambles. He even remembers his mother at this moment, but he is unable to have lively conversations with women, such as his first wife, sister and daughter anymore. He tells the audience,

> No longer did I summon up the Karens and Ediths and Mollys of my life to help brighten up the endless sleepless nights.... Now they came on their own. Uninvited. Unsummoned. Unstoppable. (*JW* 198)

He submerges completely in a world which happens inside his mind, totally he misses the real world around. He might get professional satisfaction creating something permanent on page after eight hours of effort, but at the same time he misses those eight hours in his practical life. In Act II when he feels alienated from his living wife, he imagines back his first wife and his grown up daughter Molly who questions his artistic detachment thus, "If I can create this intimacy, why can't I experience in my own life" (*JW* 217-18). He understands when she becomes one of his important characters why can't she play some important role in real life.

After such kind of scrutiny which evoke deep questions in Simon, he is able to analyze and understand why he really needs to write in such a case, when he is alienated from his surroundings. At the end of the play, he explains to his wife why he writes. It is not just because he makes his living from it but it is also because, "It's the only thing that doesn't reject me. My characters are the only ones I know who love me unconditionally, because I give them life" (*JW* 224-25). After a long journey in his life with his profession which is under his control, he is unable to desert it. Not even when Maggie or Molly develop aversion to his profession which has taken him away from them. He is like Chekov, the writer in *The Good Doctor* who simply says, "I have no choice. I am a writer."[7]

Like *Bare Foot in the Park, Chapter Two* and *Brighton Beach Memoirs*, he experiments with the events in the life and death of his first wife and breakup of his second marriage. He is critical of his own devotedness to his art of writing and his compelled feeling to write. Though he tries to pull some of his life to lead a more practical life with daughter and wife, he could not do it long and the writer in him is pulled like a magnet to indulge in writing once again.

He should have control and should sense the security and solidarity. He is more like Jake observing more and living less. In fact, Simon's third wife Diane Lander has made an agreement with him that she should never write about her or her daughter during her life time. She rather warns him "to live the relationship rather than use it as a raw material for his plays."[8]

To develop human relationships to make his life more meaningful, Jake should first cross the hurdles which are in the form of his first deceased wife and mother. Attached more to them he is not able to understand his second wife in a better light but anyway his imaginative conversations help him in coming to terms with reality. In fact, his first wife cautions him not to idealize her so much in future, "I don't want to be a shrine. I don't want to be a touched-up photo in a family album" (*JW* 214).

His mother lurks deep inside his conscience and as Susan Koprince recognizes, it is obvious in his fears:

1. His fear of abandonment (when he was five he awoke from a nap to discover that his mother was gone).
2. His fear of being controlled (she used to tie him into his chair with a rope).
3. According to Brain Rhinehart, even his fear of castration (revealed in the fantasy about his toe being sucked down the drain).[9]

Simon reflects the American world of his time. After analyzing himself thus and when self-discovery occurs he hears a voice saying, "I love you...and I forgive you" (*JW* 227). He realizes with some amazement that it is what he wanted to say his mother and it is this kind of approach that may bridge his relationship with his second wife Maggie. Thus, the play ends with a positive note. When he tries to live a real life with Maggie who returns to his apartment to make up the differences. They both meet on the stairs, "like God and Adam reaching out in the Sistine Chapel" (*JW* 229).

WORKS CITED

Barnes, Clive. "Everything's Jake: Neil Simon Gets Better With Time", *New York Theatre Critics' Review*, Vol. 53, 1992.

Kroll, Jack. "Simon Says: Real or False," *New York Theatre Critic's Reviews*, Vol. 53, 1992.

Koprince, Susan. *Understanding Neil Simon*, Columbia: University of South Carolina Press, 2002.

Mclean Jr. Albert, *American Vaudeville as Ritual. Lexington*: University of Kentucky Press, 1965.

Rhinehart, Brian and Norman N. Holland, "Jake's Women: A dialogue," *Neil Simon: A Case Book*, ed. Gary Konas.

Richards, David. *The Last of the Red-Hot Playwrights*, New York: Times. 1991.

Simon, Neil. "The Good Doctor", *The Collected Plays of Neil Simon*, Vol. 2, New York: Plume, 1979.

Simon, Neil. "Jake's Women", *The Collected Plays of Neil Simon*, Vol. 4, New York: Touchstone, 1998.

8

Hoax of the American Dream in Bernard Malamud's *The Assistant*

Rupali Mirza

ABSTRACT

Bernard Malamud is a widely-acclaimed writer in the field of Jewish-American Literature. Malamud's works have an underlying theme of familial relationships along with loss and suffering. In the situation after the Second World War, Jews left their homeland, which caused a lot of suffering and anguish to them but at the same time, they never lost their belief in their true fate, moral values and traditions. Malamud has been able to evolve the unique idea behind the identity of an individual, what he is and what he should be. In order to achieve the latter, the hero of Malamud undergoes a spiritual growth which helps him to understand the deeper truths of life. It was the time of industrialization when people had almost forgotten their folkways and mores. In such an atmosphere, gain of material wealth is what mattered most to them. In other words, the "American Dream" of success and prosperity is what everyone was looking upto. In this background, the purpose of Malamud's writings was to save the culture from the present state of degradation by setting up examples as that of Morris Bober, who flourished in spiritual and moral growth in spite of material and financial emptiness and lack of prosperity and exposed the great sham behind the "American Dream".

Keywords: Sham, American Dream, Loss, Suffering, Alienation.

The Assistant by Bernard Malamud highlights the inequality prevalent in the American society in terms of race, class and ethnicity which makes the American Dream unreachable. The idea of the American Dream preaches that success is for anyone who can do hard work but this concept seems to be a hoax as far as practical implications of it are concerned. In *The Assistant*, Morris Bober is the protagonist who upholds jewish values and always abides by them. However, his wish to run his grocery business only through righteous means becomes a potential threat on his way to financial progress, also his ideas of Judaism help him further never to be dishonest. Despite of all his positive and righteous ideas about life, Morris is never able to attain the success which the American Dream promised. This was largely because of his ethnic origin too as Jews belonged to one of the marginalized communities which were kept out of the mainframe of the promising American Dream.

The novel speaks of two completely different characters, Morris Bober who stands for jewish values and honesty in all his life's endeavours, as opposed to Frank Alpine who uses all fair and fowl means to have material gains. It is the same grocery store which suffers losses in a regular course when run by Morris but when Frank looks after it, business becomes profitable. This talks a lot about the shortcomings of the American society which cared little for values of honesty and integrity which are represented by Morris. They cared more for achieving quick success even though if it was gained through fraudulent means. The idealistic vision of the American Dream projected the view of a society which was devoid of class divisions. In reality, this picture is hardly true as the society was divided on the basis of gender, religion, race and ethnicity. The people of foreign origin as well as women were considered to be a part of the marginalized section of the society. Morris stands alone upholding his moral values in a completely valueless society which cares little for his ideas of morality. The irony of the situation is that the society makes him believe that he was a complete failure in his life. However, if deep analysis is conducted, it was Morris who was able to gain real success through his life of morality and righteousness. Morris considered himself to be a failure, misguided and totally given into the misgivings of the American Dream society.

People like Julius Karp, who also belonged to the Jewish community are more acceptable in the American society because they are able to imbibe the values of the completely valueless society and did not try hard to achieve anything more than material wealth. Frank Alpine is a Roman Catholic who, however, does not abide by what his religion preached. He became closer to Morris in realizing that religion was just a way of life and it had deeper connotations where practicing what one preaches had more value. Morris has less buyers for his righteous ideas as his own daughter Helen and his wife, Ida don't respect his ideas. Ida tries to persuade her daughter Helen to be friendly towards Nat more due to his financial success than for the reason that he was also a jew and so he belonged to the same community as them. Ida also doesn't have much regard for her husband's principles and values which she considered shallow and of little practical use. In fact, she knew that Morris's principles were the cause of his failure. Her ideas had been totally corrupted by the ideas and ideals of the American Dream society. A man can overlook criticism of his ideas by the society but he is unable to bear the criticism of his ideals by his own family. It was when Ida, his wife and Helen, his own daughter rejected his idealism, their behavior echoed by the entire society, Morris accepted himself as a complete failure.

Frank Alpine, *The Assistant* of Morris comes out of his own shell of baser morals and tries to imbibe Morris's high ideals. Other Jews of the community such as Julius Karp and Nat Pearl lose their intrinsic values of being a true jew by not adhering to the doctrine of Judaism. They go further to adopt the false values and principles of materialism which are not a part of the jewish way of life. This ensures their survival in the American society as they are not true jews in spite of their same ethnic origin as Morris and therefore they are acceptable in the society which not only is tolerant towards them but also helps them to flourish in spite of their origin.

The school of Marxist Criticism believes that it is economic power which drives all institutions. Marx believed that:

> The production of ideas, concepts and consciousness is first of all directly interwoven with the material intercourse of man, the language of real life. Conceiving, thinking and the real intercourse of men, appear here as the direct efflux of men's material behaviour. The same applies to mental production as expressed in the language of the politics, laws, morality, religion, and metaphysics, of a people. Men are producers of their conceptions, ideas etc.—real, active men, as they are conditioned by a definite development of their productive forces and of the intercourse corresponding to these, up to its furthest forms. (qtd. in Nagarajan, 223)

Thus, the American society believed in its set goals and ideas for the achievement of wealth. As said by Marx, their consciousness, culture and ideas were also influenced by their need for material wealth. They were unable to acknowledge the ideas of morality, honesty and righteousness, personified by the character of Morris Bober. He had no place in a society which was completely based on notions of profitability. His counterparts such as Julius Karp became rich and successful only because they compromised with their values. Julius invested his money to open a liquor store, Morris, however, could not go against his principles to invest in such an immoral trade. Any power structure implies that politics, laws, religion as well as notions of morality are determined by those who hold the purse strings. Thus, the American society did not allow those to be successful who did not adhere to their valueless system.

Engels believed that "repressive ideology" is "false consciousness" as the ideas in reality are in opposition to the "material reality". Such repressive ideology is circulated by the ruling classes to influence the set of beliefs of the people due to which people are deceived. The American Dream is one such ideology which was sowed among the middle-class society to make them believe that through hard work they could become rich:

> It is a power ideology meant for legitimizing and perpetuating the interests of the privileged ruling class. Ideology promotes false class consciousness. Patriotism, religion, individualism, consumerism are all the different manifestations of repressive bourgeois ideology. (Nagarajan 226)

It was the same "repressive ideology" which influenced the multi-cultural society of *The Assistant.* People like Morris Bober fell prey to such notions of gaining prosperity through hard work. Little did they realize that it was just a trap laid by the ruling class.

The first Jews in America came in mid-1600s. They came in a small ship and settled on the eastern coast in the Dutch colony of Massachusetts. It was from then onwards that the Jews started migrating to the land of new opportunities, especially from the European continent. The Jews were mainly a trading community and they conducted their business as "peddlars". They usually carried a big sack on their back from which they sold goods of utility. The Jewish trade prospered in due course of time creating ever-lasting brands such as Levi Strauss & Co. which began in 1853 in San Francisco, California. This trading population was mostly that of German Jews who opted for stationary business apart from peddling. The American bourgouis capitalism allowed and rather appreciated the business efforts that the Jews made for their settlement in the new land. It was a free-for-all economy where Jews could conduct business as they wanted. This immigration came to a hault with the Immigration Act of 1924. This Act was introduced in order to limit the ever-growing population of the United States as it had already become the most promising land for anyone who wanted to achieve success. Morris Bober was one such Jewish immigrant who runs a grocery store which becomes the reason for his plight. In a capitalistic environment everyone thought of earning money without caring about the means he used for it, unlike Morris who never compromised on his honesty. This was the main reason for his failure as described by Malamud:

> The grocer, on the other hand, had never altered his fortune, unless degrees of poverty meant alteration, for luck and he were, if not natural enemies, not good friends. He labored long hours, was the soul of honesty—he could not escape his honesty, it was bedrock; to cheat would cause an explosion in him, yet he trusted cheaters—coveted nobody's nothing and always got poorer. The harder he worked—his toil was a form of time devouring time—the less he seemed to have. He was Morris Bober and could be nobody more fortunate. With that name you had no sure sense of property, as if it were in your blood and history not to possess, or if by some miracle to own something, to do so on the verge of loss. At the end you were sixty and had less than at thirty. (Malamud, 16)

The major characters in *The Assistant* are based in the New York City. All of them are in a state of constant suffering to achieve the American Dream. Julius Karp is not considered an honorable man, though he had climbed up the social ladder economically. Nat Pearl, a prospective match for Morris's daughter, Helen, speaks Yiddish but has acquired education at Columbia and at the law school. Putting aside the success stories in the same community, there is a long story of Bobers who have little for their subsistence in spite of owning a grocery store. The possibility of becoming rich and successful had drawn Morris to Brooklyn. Morris being an owner of a small, dilapidated grocery is unable to make use of any opportunities which come his way for attaining success or making quick profits. He continues to struggle trying to realize the American Dream. He had lost his son, Ephraim and at the same time he had also lost the ability to provide financial settlement for his family to the extent that he is unable to send his daughter, Helen to the university due to the shortage of money. *The Assistant* is the story of both Frank Alpine and Morris Bober. The former is an Italian drifter who happens to conduct a robbery at Morris' grocery during closing time. Frank hit Morris' head with a pistol but after much pursuation and domination they were not able to find much money in the till. Frank realizes his mistake and as an act of seeking forgiveness, asks Morris to give him a job at the grocery store. Morris allows Frank to take care of the grocery due to two reasons, firstly the former's condition as a homeless drifter and secondly, his own condition, as his wound was bleeding and he could not run the store on his own. Frank's offer as an assistant proved to be a lucrative option for Morris under his present circumstances. The only pre-condition that he had to fulfill was to secure food and shelter for Frank.

The setting of the novel is in the late 1940s and early 1950s, in Brooklyn, New York. It is a Jewish-American as well as modern American novel. It is narrated by an omniscient narrator. Much of what Malamud wrote came from his own life's experiences. *The Assistant* was the second novel of Malamud. He grew up in Brooklyn and spent his youthful years running a grocery store owned by his father. The story of Morris Bober is inspired by his own business. He completed his graduation from Erasmus High School. The Wall Street Crash leading to The Great Depression formed a background of financial crisis in his literary works. He completed his B.A. in 1936 and accomplished a Master's degree from Columbia University. In the beginning, after completion of his education, he taught night classes in Erasmus Hall High School. Malamud became a faculty at Oregon State University where he taught for many years and later moved on to teach at Bennington College. Malamud was influenced by I.B. Singer and Isaac Babel. Malamud wrote many works including; *The Natural, The Assistant, A New Life, The Fixer, Pictures of Fidelman, The Tenants, Rembrandt's Hat, Dubin's Lives, God's Grace, Idiots First* and many short stories. Most of Malamud's heroes are men of high moral standards and responsibility as discussed by Helterman:

> Suffering, commitment and responsibility are the hallmarks of Malamud's heroes. They are men who start with nothing before some system tries to make them into less than nothing. The greatest of these heroes grow stronger as their lives become more minimal. It is here suffering ennobles by building commitment to an ideal. Sometimes the ideal has independent validity, but more

> often the commitment itself gives an act its moral value. These acts of heroism at their best, are not acts of self, but derive from or create responsibility towards another human being.
>
> Always the characters find themselves morally linked to each other. Not only do the weak, like Frank Alpine in *The Assistant*, find themselves supporting the weaker (Bober), more surprisingly, the oppressors find themselves prisoners of their victims' determination. Grubeshov, the prosecutor in *The Fixer*, is in fact less free than his prisoner, and ends up begging Bok to compromise. Gilley, who holds the fate of Levin in his hands, is the one who ends up with no choices. And the tenants in the novel of that name, finds that despite their mutual hatred, they can do nothing without each other. (Helterman, 8)

The early years of Malamud's life also form the reason why he chose to write for human suffering. He was a motherless child as he lost the care of his mother only when he was fourteen years of age. He and his elder brother were raised by their father who ran a small grocery store and depended completely on it for their subsistence. This meager income helped Malamud understand the greater concerns of life such as love and suffering which were spiritually greater issues than the acquisition of material wealth. The protagonist of Malamud, Frank Alpine in *The Assistant* begins to understand the same concerns as he slowly evolves when he undergoes a complete inner change which helps him to grow from an individual having only limited perspective. This growth helps him to become a part of the bigger picture where he could see his contribution to human existence. He is able to understand how worldly suffering can elevate the man morally and that his material failure or his failure in attaining wealth did not affect his growth as a moralistic man. This was precisely the reason why Malamud thought that the promise of material success made by the American Dream was not enough to make a man truly successful. Malamud sometimes addresses himself as "a real child of Depression". The Great Depression of 1929 better known as The Wall Street Crash was a crash of the American stock market and in turn crash of the entire American economy which brought a slump in the American market. People lost their jobs due to recession and business suffered. Malamud himself worked in a yarn manufacturing factory and led a tough life. Most of his characters lead a similar life which is devoid of comfort. The life of his characters is full of suffering so that they may learn the inner concerns of human existence. Malamud is always called a Jewish-American writer, although his reason was choosing Jewish characters is that he is able to project them better but through the Jewish experience he wants to address larger concerns of humanity and not just those concerns which are intrinsically related to Jews only.

WORKS CITED

Abramson, Edward A. *Bernard Malamud Revisited.* New York: Twayne Publishers, 1993.

Alter, Iska. *The Good Man's Dilemma: Social Criticism in the Fiction of Bernard Malamud.* New York: AMS Press, 1981.

Astro, Richard, and Benson, Jackson J., eds. *The Fiction of Bernard Malamud.* Corvallis: Oregon State University Press, 1977.

Bloom Harold, ed. *Bernard Malamud.* New York: Chelsea House Publishers, 1986.

Cohen, Sandy. *Bernard Malamud and the Trial by Love.* Amsterdam: Rodopi. N.V., 1974.

Cotkin, George. "French Existentialism and American Popular Culture: 1945-1948." *The Historian*, Vol. 61: 2, 1999.

Ducharme, Robert. *Art and Idea in the Novels of Bernard Malamud: Toward the Fixer.* The Hague: Mouton, 1974.

Fiedler, Leslie. *To the Gentiles.* New York: Stein and Day, 1972.

Field, Leslie A. and Joyce W., eds. *Bernard Malamud and the Critics.* New York: New York University Press, 1970.

Field, Leslie A. and Joyce W., eds. *Bernard Malamud: A Collection of Critical Essays.* Englewood Cliffs, New Jersey: Prentice Hall, 1975.

Fleming, Ed and Gunn, Albert E. "European Existentialism." *The Review of Metaphysics*, Vol. 52: 2, 1998.

Furman, Andrew. "Imagining Jews, Imagining Gentiles: A New Look at Saul Bellow's *The Victim* and Bernard Malamud's *The Assistant.*" *A Significant Pattern*. Daniel Walden, ed. Vol. 16, 1997.

Girgus, Sam. *The New Convenant: Jewish Writers and the American Idea*. Chapel Hill: University of North Carolina Press, 1984.

Guttmann, Allen. *The Jewish Writer in America: Assimilation and the Crisis of Identity.* New York: Oxford University Press, 1971.

Helterman, Jeffrey. "Bernard Malamud." In *Dictionary of Literary Biography: American Novelists Since World War II,* Vol. 2, edited by Jeffrey Helterman and Richard Layman, 291-304. Detroit: Gale Research Company, 1978.

Helterman, Jeffrey. *Understanding Bernard Malamud.* Columbia: University of South Carolina Press, 1985.

Hershinow, Sheldon J. *Bernard Malamud.* New York: Frederick Ungar Publishing Company, 1980.

Knopp, Josephine Z. *The Trial of Judaism in Contemporary Jewish Writing.* Urbana: University of Illinois Press, 1975.

Lasher, Lawrence M. *Conversations with Bernard Malamud.* Jackson: University Press of Mississippi, 1991.

Malin, Irving. *Jews and Americans.* Carbondale: Southern Illinois University Press, 1965.

Malin, Irving, ed. *Contemporary American-Jewish Literature: Critical Essays.* Bloomington: Indiana University Press, 1973.

Moore, Harry T. ed. *Contemporary American Novelists.* Carbondale.: Southern Illinois University Press, 1964.

Richman, Sidney. *Bernard Malamud.* New York: Twayne, 1966. Good general study of the first half of Malamud's career.

Roth, Philip. "Imagining Jews." In *Reading My Self and Others,* edited by Philip Roth, 215-46. London: Jonathan Cape, 1975.

Salz berg, Joel. *Critical Essays on Bernard Malamud.* Boston: G.K. Hall and Co., 1987.

Schulz, Max F. *Radical Sophistication: Studies in Contemporary Jewish-American Novelists.* Athens: Ohio University Press, 1969.

9

Poetics of a Dream Deferred: Langston Hughes's Poetic Sociology

Subashish Bhattacharjee and *Saikat Guha*

ABSTRACT

Any historification of the chronology of American literature is incomplete without an extensive impetus on the literature originating from the African Americans. Especially in the context of twenty-first century American literature, it can be observed that the manifest and tacit influence of African American literature has been profoundly felt in terms of technique, ideology and socio-cultural schematics. While the origins of African American literature could be traced from the slave narrative, it was the Harlem Renaissance that led to an upsurge in literature of the African Americans. The poetry of Langston Hughes, the unofficial poet laureate of the movement, has been widely influential in the creation of a specific African American poetics, replete with its own linguistic maneuvers and tropes, its blues and jazz-inspired musicality and rhythm that absorbed Harlem, the wider African American culture with its distinct hues, and its social marginalization and sense of victimhood. The following paper looks at the early phase of Hughes's poetic career during which he displays his anguish and disdain over the racist overtures of the predominantly White America in such remarkable poems as "Democracy" and "The Negro Speaks of

Rivers," and his landmark essay, "The Negro Artist and the Racial Mountain," and how he provides the socio-literary underpinnings of the Black Aesthetic and Black Power movements.

Keywords: Socio-cultural, Jazz-inspired, Marginalization, Afro-Americans.

Literature of the Blacks or African Americans occupies a large part in the corpus of American literature which is "colored" with its distinctive hues. Since Columbus's discovery of the New World in 1492, the African surge has lashed the shores of America. The Africans were forcibly brought in America as slaves to work in the colonial plantations and agriculture. The official abolition of slavery in 1863 by the President Abraham Lincoln was only the beginning of a protracted, agonizing journey which the African Americans had to embark upon to obtain equality and justice. The first exposition of the oppression and repression of the African Americans was illustrated in the slave narratives as late as the nineteenth century (Stowe's classic *Uncle Tom's Cabin* was published as a book in 1852). It was only at the beginning of the twentieth century that the African Americans started decrying the racial discrimination in a characteristic voice of their own. The first major juncture at which the African Americans gained literary attention, not only of their own community but also that of the White majority, was the Harlem Renaissance outbreak in a quarter of Manhattan which reached its peak during the 1920s. The chief socio-political and cultural activists who gave impetus to the movement were WEB Du Bois and Alain Locke while its unofficial poet laureate was Langston Hughes. Although the literary artists were not guided by a philosophy as such, cites Catherine Morley, they were "linked, however, by a common black experience and the desire for self-definition and self-expression" (196).

The twentieth century witnessed the rise of what Locke calls "the New Negro" as opposed to "the Old Negro" who had been "more of a myth than a man" and "a stock figure perpetuated as an historical *fiction* partly in innocent sentimentalism, partly in deliberate reactionism" ("Enter the New Negro", emphasis added). The mind of the New Negro, observes Locke, "seems suddenly to have slipped from under the tyranny of social intimidation and to be shaking off the psychology of imitation and implied inferiority" (*ibid.*). The intelligent New Negro is audacious enough to break free from the manacles of racial discrimination and actively takes part in the assertion of the African American heritage whose inner objectives should be to renovate a damaged group psychology. The making of a truly "democratic" America, according to Locke, would not be possible but for the participation of the Negros in it. Langston Hughes voiced the similar concern in his poetry by summoning a true democratic spirit to America which segregates the African Americans on the alleged ground of inferiority and dependence. The injustice to the African Americans merely prohibits the materialization of the tenets of democracy further, as Hughes says in the poem "Democracy":

Democracy will not come
Today, this year
Nor ever
Through compromise and fear.

I have as much right
As the other fellow has
To stand
On my two feet
And own the land.

The sense of belonging can never be attained by the Blacks with compromise-formation. Inspired by an ardent Marxist-socialist spirit, Hughes argues in favor of equality and justice to his community. He writes with the sense of a victim to whom America was never a cozy home to live in:

(It never was America to me.)
O, let my land be a land where Liberty
Is crowned with no false patriotic wreath,
But opportunity is real, and life is free,

Equality is in the air we breathe.
(There's never been equality for me,
Nor freedom in this "homeland of the free.") ("Let America")

The phrase "homeland of the free" appears to be an ironic phrase to the poet which fails to signify anything substantial to him. An invisible prison has kept the African-Americans captive which forbids them realize the logic of freedom but without it no one can triumph over the existential crisis, as Hughes says, "I live here, too/ I want freedom/ Just as you" ("Democracy"). The emancipation from these subjections, in Hughes's literary-practical philosophy, is possible through the conduit of an expressive medium—Art. And the specific art which he emphasizes upon is unquestionably poetry. Unlike other "theorists" of poetic measures, Hughes embodied his mannerisms in his poetry, as Arnold Rampersad insists, Hughes's poetry was "the sum of the often troubled and troubling parts that racism compelled him to play as a writer and as a black man seeking to live almost exclusively by his writings. [...] To love his work is not to insist on the obsolescence of older, whiter versions of tradition" ("Foreword" x-xi).

During his long eventful life Langston Hughes produced several volumes of writing which fall into different literary and poetic genres. We, however, would limit our discussion here to the early poetry of Hughes which illustrates his bitterness against racism in America. Apart from his indignant criticism of the racial prejudices of the predominantly White America his poems also encompass the nuances of African American identity which gained optimistic stimulus from the age-old folklore. Hughes's poetic sensibility is steeped in the root of the Negro community, that is, their African heritage which he captures in a commemorative whim. His poetry is "an act of celebration, demonstrating a kind of racial pride in its vibrant images and throbbing rhythmical pulse" (Morley 201). And Hughes draws not merely in theme but also in technique and influence from the innate traditions of Black culture in a way that absorbs the influences without eclipsing them in affect of importance. Harold Bloom too has noted: "Folk traditions ranging from blues to spirituals to jazz songs to work chants to many other modes do get into Hughes's poetry, but his poems on the whole do not compare adequately to the best instances of those cultural models" (1). The absorption of such measures is not blatantly evident, but subtly locatable in the images and metaphors Hughes employs to specify an African American consciousness. In such poems as "The Negro Speaks of Rivers," Hughes compares his soul with that of a river—"My soul has grown deep like the rivers." The characteristic quality of a river which flows through different lands and dissolves boundaries is like the poet's soul embracing all the rebuffs that come in its way. His soul, like the river, is sacred and all-embracing which bears witness to the labyrinths of history:

> I bathed in the Euphrates when dawns were young.
> I built my hut near the Congo and it lulled me to sleep.
> I looked upon the Nile and raised the pyramids above it.
> I heard the singing of the Mississippi when Abe Lincoln
> went down to New Orleans, and I've seen its muddy
> bosom turn all golden in the sunset. ("Negro Speaks")

Arnold Rampersad has remarkably elucidated the symbolic breath of the poem thus:

> The muddy river is his [Hughes's] race, the primal source out of which he is born anew; on that "muddy bosom" of the race as black mother, or grandmother, he rests secure forever. The angle of the sun on the muddy water is like the angle of a poet's vision, which turns mud into gold. ("On 'The Negro...' ")

Although a close associate of Du Bois during his propagation of the New Negro ideals, Hughes differed from the former with regard to his addressees. Du Bois was elitist in his ideas such as the "Talented Tenth"—a group of university-educated Black men—who were considered by him to be the representative of the African American community which they should voice. On the other hand, Hughes was a poet of the masses whose life he closely observed and captured in his poetry. He writes in his famous essay "The Negro Artist and the Racial Mountain" that the "high-class" Negro who is born and raised in an affluent African American family is ashamed of his roots. He tries to ape the manners and arts of the White, which he considers to be the yardstick of standard mode of living. Hughes cites a number of examples in the essay which illustrate the fear of the Negro artist to define himself in his own idioms. Rather he prefers to look at himself through the eyes of the White which Du Bois calls "double consciousness"—the "sense of always looking at one's self through the eyes of others, of measuring one's soul by the tape of a world that looks on in amused contempt and pity" (Du Bois 869). Hughes cites a certain aspiring Negro poet who proclaimed "I want to be a poet—not a Negro poet" which Hughes finds harmful for the success of the man as an artist "for no great poet has ever been afraid of being himself" ("Negro Artist"). But at the same time, Hughes acknowledges the racial mountain that stands in the way as great obstruction to the success of the Black poets—"this urge within the race toward whiteness, the desire to pour racial individuality into the mold of American standardization, and to be as little Negro and as much American as possible" (*ibid.*). Hughes's substitution of "American" for the White is interesting as it caustically posits the dividing lines between the White and the Black—the later being an "invisible man". When the Negro poets write their writings are considered inferior in comparison to that of the White poets. Books written by Negro writers seldom find a White reader. What most surprises Hughes is the irony that the African American community, instead of admiring the Negro poetry which sings their communal ethos, maintains a certain distance from it because they are afraid of admiring it. Their subconscious idea "white is best", observes Hughes, which is infused in them by a predatory White culture, education, morals, religion and so on, makes them disdain their own heritage as something inferior and childish. He cherishes the same belief as that of Du Bois that the New Negro, who is awakened to new sense of *beauty*, *truth* and *justice*, can perform miracles.

We black folk may help for we have within us as a race new stirrings; stirrings of the beginning of a new appreciation of joy, of a new desire to create, of a new will to be; as though in this morning of group life we had awakened from some sleep that at once dimly mourns the past and dreams a splendid future [...] (Du Bois, "Criteria").

The confluence of anguish and the desire to carve out an identity independent of the mores of White-ness is expressed in a manner quite aggressive and oppositionary. The locus of Hughes's essay has been summed up in the words of Arnold Rampersad quite aptly:

> When Hughes opened his greatest essay, "The Negro Artist and the Racial Mountain" (1926) by equating the desire of a certain young black poet to be seen as nothing but a poet with the desire to be white, he was stating his understanding of the most complex problem facing the young black writer. [...] the domination of white poetic standards through the many unquestionably alluring volumes of white verse, backed ultimately by the domination of white culture, effectively made their dilemma forbiddingly close to that of a racial death-wish described by Hughes at the start of the essay. ("Langston Hughes's *Fine Clothes*" 8)

Though critical of the racist bias of America which so often denigrates the African Americans, Hughes represents himself as a part of this "flawed" country in "I, Too":

> I, too, sing America.
>
> I am the darker brother.

This poem, which is modeled on Whitman's poem "I Hear America Singing," adds what Whitman overlooks—that the Negros too sing of America which has been their home for centuries. Hughes is quite temperate in this poem and believes that there will come a time when the White will appreciate his inner beauty and feel ashamed of mistreating him:

> They'll see how beautiful I am
>
> And be ashamed—
>
> I, too, am America. ("I, Too")

In such poems as "I Continue to Dream" he registers his indifference to the approval of the White of his dreams. He is aware that the dream will not come true overnight, but he is hopeful nevertheless:

Do you understand my dreams?
Sometimes you say you do,
And sometimes you say you don't.
Either way it doesn't matter.
I continue to dream.

Hughes is aware of the different forms of racial-profiling rampant in America, as Delgado and Stephancic list in their invaluable "critical race theory": everyday racism, interest convergence, social construction of race, differential racialization, intersectionality and a unique voice of color. The African-American people suffer from racial discrimination in their everyday lives which is invariably a result of misconstrued Social Darwinism. There is no genetic proof of inferiority by way of which the African Americans are characterized, but race is socially constructed to serve the interests of the White Americans to keep the African Americans subservient. It also serves the interest of the White to racialize the dark "others" to gain utmost privilege from this dominance, as is demonstrated in Hughes's poem "The Ballad of the Landlord". The poem faithfully portrays the twofold exploitation of an African American tenant by his White landlord who exploits him for financial benefits and then convicts him on a concocted accusation that his former has tried to kill him with the trifling cause of poor condition of the tenement. In a bitter satirical tone, Hughes records the imposed gravity on the trifling incident:

Police! Police!
Come and get this man!
He's trying to ruin the government
And overturn the land! ("Ballad")

Even though Hughes is not considered to be an immaculate craftsman of poetry, it is his raw sensibility that ensured prolonged relevance of his poetry as opposed to that of several other practitioners who have been relegated to obscurity over the decades since the Harlem Renaissance. Harold Bloom states:

The refusal (to abide or end in alienation) may be ascribed to Hughes's profound, almost selfless love for his own people, and makes him an authentic and heroic exemplar for many subsequent black American writers. Whatever the inadequacies of Hughes's various styles, his place in literary history is an assured one (2).

There is very little to add by way of conclusion to Langston Hughes's embodiment of the social and cultural ethos of "blackness" in America in the literature that developed during and after he wrote. Hughes's poetic credibility lies in the fact that he not only produced the tenets of African American poetic production but also inspired future generations of poets to rigorously employ them in further varying forms. We may attempt to produce an assessment of Hughes's importance in American literature by means of an eulogizing remark by Tidwell and Ragar that places him beyond the singularly monolithic purviews of biography, African Americanness and American historicity:

> His [Hughes's] death, in 1967, represented the end of one era and the beginning of a new one. In the younger generation, a new spirit of proclaiming the beauty of blackness emerged and replaced the anti-Euro-American rhetoric. Like rivers remembering their sources, these insurgents ultimately came to understand and applaud the social commitments of their predecessors. Their own writing revised the ahistorical premises of their earlier aesthetic and paid homage to their forebears for doing courageous cultural work. One of the principals so honored was Langston Hughes. (12)

WORKS CITED

Bloom, Harold. "Introduction." *Langston Hughes*. Ed. Harold Bloom. New York: Infobase, 2008. 1-3.

Delgado, Richard and Jean Stefancic. *Critical Race Theory: An Introduction*. New York: New York University Press, 2001.

Du Bois, W.E.B. "Criteria of Negro Art." *The Crisis* 32 (1926). Web. *WEBDuBois.org*. 1 May 2015. <http://www.webdubois.org/dbCriteriaNArt.html>

——. "The Souls of Black Folk." *Literary Theory: An Anthology*. Ed. Julie Rivkin and Michael Ryan. Oxford: Blackwell Publishers, 1998. 868-72.

Hughes, Langston. "The Negro Artist and the Racial Mountain." *The Nation* (1926). Web. *Modern American Poetry*. 1 May 2015. <http://www.english.illinois.edu/maps/poets/g_l/hughes/mountain.htm>

Locke, Alain. "Enter the New Negro." *Survey Graphic* (1925). Web. *National Humanities Center Resource Toolbox*. 1 May 2015. <http://nationalhumanitiescenter.org/pds/maai3/migrations/text8/lockenewnegro.pdf>

Morley, Catherine. *Modern American Literature*. Edinburgh: Edinburgh University Press, 2012.

Neal, Larry. "The Black Arts Movement." *Drama Review* (1968). Web. *National Humanities Center Resource Toolbox*. 1 May 2015. <http://nationalhumanitiescenter.org/pds/maai3/community/text8/blackartsmovement.pdf>

"On 'The Negro Speaks of Rivers'." Web. *Modern American Poetry*. Web. 1 May 2015. <http://www.english.illinois.edu/maps/poets/g_l/hughes/rivers.htm>

Rampersad, Arnold. "Foreword." *Montage of a Dream: The Art and Life of Langston Hughes*. Eds. John Edgar Tidwell and Cheryl R. Ragar. Columbia: University of Missouri Press, 2007. ix-xii.

——. "Langston Hughes's *Fine Clothes to the Jew*." *Langston Hughes*. Ed. Harold Bloom. New York: Infobase, 2008. 5-21.

Tidwell, John Edgar and Cheryl R. Ragar. "Langston Hughes Revisited and Revised: An Introduction." *Montage of a Dream: The Art and Life of Langston Hughes*. Eds. John Edgar Tidwell and Cheryl R. Ragar. Columbia: University of Missouri Press, 2007. 1-15.

Note: All of Hughes's poems have been cited in the website PoetryNook.com on 1 May 2015. <www.poetrynook.com>

10

Murdering "American Dream": Murder in Norman Mailer's *An American Dream* (1965)

Anindya Sundar Polley

ABSTRACT

America's involvement in World Wars and the nation's emergence as a new superpower highly affected its society, culture and consciousness of the common masses and America's ethnic and racial character underwent significant transformation as an outcome. In America, since the 20th century, feelings of skepticism, alienation, and a general trend that negativated the earlier orthodox, humane and moral outlook started predominating. People started to see things in the parameter of the complex mindset, as the public confidence received a heavy jolt by seeing the failure of the 'American Dream'. America's post-war economic gains alone could not undo the scenario and people started to live in newer insecurities on every new day, which got an outlet in their evil actions.

The novel which is selected for the current analysis offers significant insight into the aforesaid scenario. The ideology driven murder committed by the protagonist Rojack is the central motif of the novel which forces to arise several questions—is it the physical resistance of Rojack which ultimately ends in the form of murder is a pragmatic exercise on part of the antihero to balance the failure of his American Dream? Or is it in this process he is actually destroying his American Dream? How much can we blame the ideology in the exercise of individual lunatics? The current paper with a detailed investigation of the novel, tries to seek answers of the aforesaid questions.

Keywords: American Dream, Power, Ideology, Failure, Murder, An American Dream.

"One has to look in the eye of violence to see its meaning."
—Norman Mailer, 1967, interview for *Newsday*

'American Dream' is an idea which promises that everyone in the United States has the chance to achieve success and prosperity. And needless to say, the idea, despite of this Utopian promise, remains way behind the ultimate result, thanks to the complex socio-political scenario. America despite of her vast post-war gains (economic profit, political power, etc.), fails to capitalize it and for the people of America, the 'American Dream' remains as a myth. The case of Rojack of Mailer's *An American Dream* is no exception.

The case of Stephen Richards Rojack of Norman Mailer's *An American Dream* is fascinating and offers ample potential for our current discussion. Rojack, an apparently successful person in the socio-economic arena, is a desolate and gloom-stricken person in his personal life and is a victim of an unhappy marriage. *An American Dream* is the story of an unachieved dream of a power-loving person who wanted to use his marriage to climb the social order but fails miserably. The accidental murder where the victim Rojack suddenly becomes the killer completes this misery and Rojack's American Dream remains unfulfilled. Nunez rightly opines, "Rojack is thus the embodiment of the American dream and its subsequent degeneration into a series of nightmares. Norman Mailer depicts the postwar spiritual vacuum that Eliot in *The Waste Land* and Fitzgerald in *The Great Gatsby* describe so well" (169).

Stephen Rojack leads a glorious life before the beginning of his topsy-turvy life of unending misery. On every new day, he is living his dream and is reaching his success. He has almost charmed everybody with his charismatic individuality. Rojack is a war hero; he earns his livelihood as a Professor of Existential Psychology; he is a popular author; he is a glamorous television talk show host; and last but not least, he is an ex-Congressman. He belongs to a world where everybody dreams an American dream and he is of no exception. As a power-loving individual, he uses his marriage with Deborah Kelley [who is the daughter of the fabulously wealthy and politically influential Barney Oswald Kelly] as a ladder to move up in the social order. He confesses that her wealth and power are the motive of his love for and marriage to Deborah: "I loved her rile way a drum majorette loved the power of the band for the swell it gave to each little strut" (25). After his marriage to her, he feels strong and powerful and "with her beside" he is "one of the more active figures of the city" (25). However, soon he discovers that his marriage to Deborah is only a gift and that "the gift was only up for a loan" (26). His ambition of becoming a powerful person also hinders due to the unhappy married life, where slowly he is pushed towards the margin, Deborah taking the central stage. He fathoms the failure of his individual charisma and he does not discover an alternative way to redeem it back. His realization that he "is finally a failure" (15) in life makes him depressed and he unsuccessfully attempts suicide twice. Just like a trapped soul, he wants to come out of this confinement and the accidental murder happens out of the blue. "Her withdrawal of freedom and power from him through her separation necessitates his regaining them from her through murder. Rojack's American dream ideology of 'power' arising from his fear for Deborah's power and his disappointment ignites his idea to employ murder as a weapon to realise it" (Rajavelu 45).

Maggie McKinley perceives, "Rojack acts on a desire for total freedom from the decaying, cancerous society he envisions around him, feeling detached from the world he sees as oppressive to his individual freedom and the development of his masculine identity. For Rojack, violence functions as cleansing and cathartic force, its use justified by its potential liberating end" (162). Though he believes in high philosophies regarding death and murder like: "death was a creation more dangerous than life (14) or murder gives "vast relief and freedom but also the necessary strength and power to create a new life and a new world" (15), he doesn't 'desire' to kill Deborah, since he doesn't expect to get anything back from it. The homicide is totally unpremeditated and it is a failure of his individuality to let that happen.

Deborah, the daughter of a wealthy business tycoon, embodies the power and economic prosperity and her social position is the 'American Dream' for Rojack which he tends to achieve. Hence, when his marriage goes wrong, Rojack fears and hates his shrewish and estranged wife, Deborah. In this particular case, the desire and the failure of the desired result and the fear go hand in hand and that comes out through the outlet of unpremeditated homicide. Laura Adams remarks: "Rojack is an American archetype, who grapples with the devil to emerge victorious with a sense of fresh possibility gained from this most elemental battle" (96). In a moment of heated exchange and self-defense along with the expression of the cumulative emotions of fear, hate, fury and dejection cause a psychic imbalance in Rojack, who kills Deborah in the following manner:

> I struck her a blow on the back of the neck, a dead cold chop that dropped her to a knee, and then hooked an arm about her head and put a pressure on her throat...for ten or twenty seconds she strained in balance and then her strength began to pass, it passed over to me, and I felt my arm tightening about her neck...the arm about her neck leaped against the whisper I could feel murmuring in her throat, and crack and I choked her harder...she was dead, indeed she was dead. (35-36)

However, beside the American Dream ideology there are also various other aspects which prompts the homicide. Rojack fears his wife for her violence, for "she has once bitten his ear in a fight-making a scar" (31); for her shrewishness; for her murderous nature [Rojack fears, "I was afraid of her. She was not incapable of murdering me (Rojack)" (33)]; and for her evil powers [According to Rojack, Deborah has got some magical, evil 'power to lay a curse' (29)]. Gutman rightly observes that this 'fear' in Rojack prompts him to kill Deborah: "Rojack faces his fear and dread and commits one of the most heinous of crimes" (107). Rojack also hates her victim for her infidelity and nymphomania, for her aggressive arrogance, for her possession of wealth and power, which remains unshared with him and also for her lack of love for him. All these negative emotion collectively triggers Rojack to kill Deborah in their heated encounter.

As far as murderer's moral dilemma is concerned, Rojack, during the time of homicide, overcomes it effortlessly. He not only self-justifies his stance of killing, he also experience an act of salvation by killing his 'devilish' wife, who in her alcoholic insanity and beastly ecstasy 'charges' Rojack like a bull: "She was up like a bull, and like a bull she charged. Her head struck me (Rojack) in the stomach" (35). Gutman points out: "Deborah's veiled violence and her need for mastery and cruelty bring Rojack to a fever pitch, so that in the space of at most an hour and a half the moon guides him through a murder" (106). An unprepared Rojack does not have much time to experience/suffer his moral dilemma of whether she should have been punished or not. Rojack kills his violent wife instinctively in a reflex action. Also as a "frustrated and dejected husband deprived of wealth and power, Rojack longs to free himself from Deborah's repelling 'touch' and her 'hooks', in order to realize his American dream ideology. So, his addiction to her power makes his survival impossible during her separation from him and forces him to usurp it from her through murder" (Rajavelu 83).

Rojack's mind not only stops oscillating in dilemma at the moments of crisis, but also its status remains same immediately after the murder. He does not suffer from any negative emotion of remorse or pity, seeing the dead body of the victim; instead he experiences a satisfactory pleasure which rejuvenates his body, mind and soul: "I (Rojack) opened my eyes; I was weary with a most honorable fatigue, and my flesh seemed new, I had not felt so nice since I was twelve. It seemed inconceivable at this instant that anything in life could fail to please" (36). However, the secure stance of Rojack, which he enjoys after killing Deborah and during the time, when he lies beside her dead body, vanishes soon and the post-murder fear comes into play. Soon after the murder, he makes love with Deborah's German maid Ruta and when his excitement settles down, his rational mind experience the panic: "What the hell was I to do with Deborah (her body)? I had no solution…'keep cool, you swine', said a contemptuous voice in me, all but an echo from Deborah" (52). In his fear of getting caught, he assesses probable solutions of dumping her dead body with artistic precision and at the end decides to throw her body out of the window of the tenth floor and thus makes to look it like a simple case of suicide. However, his fear keeps on accompanying him in the form of panic until he executes his plan: "Then in a panic of strength, like desperation of getting out of a burning room, I lifted her up…and with a fever that no one see me at the open window now…I took a breath and thrust her out…" (54).

The post-murder fear, which starts with the dumping of the dead body, continues to be present with Rojack till the end. Though he almost successfully misguides the police, the detectives, the law, his influential father-in-law and though he escapes the punishment at the end and tries to realize his American dream ideology of power, freedom and material comforts, he is been haunted by this fear throughout his life. Isabella opines, "Rojack escapes from the corrupt society of the United States into the sanctuary of an unspoiled state of nature. Rojack achieves the American dream of success. But the price he pays is too large" (70). In the limited encounters with detectives, he behaves more like a convicted criminal due to this dread, though no substantial proof has been produced against him. Rojack suffers within, thanks to this fear and this affects his post-murder life to a large extent.

As far as the action of Rojack is concerned, it creates an ambiguous situation. Is he murdering his 'American Dream' or is he actually doing the redemption through it? And it raises serious questions to Mailer's intention. Rojack's craving for an influential, stable, social position, on one hand is thwarted by his instinctual action of killing Deborah. Is it not a misnomer of achieving the 'American Dream'? On the other hand, the success, Rojack enjoys after killing his wife after hoodwinking the law and escaping out of America, is so limited, that it can't at all be called 'success'. At this point, Cyrus Ernesto Zirakzadeh's comment is most pertinent, who points out "The search for an unambiguous and stable social structure is, ironically, psychologically destabilizing, according to Mailer. Because humans are partly animalistic, they naturally enjoy physical challenges, risks, and thrills. In the absence of such outlets, they become anxious and restless and satisfy their feral desires vicariously" (637).

The title of the novel also demands justification. Is this 'An American Dream' is a mere individual success dream? Or is it a collective dream of the population of the whole nations, who chase it like a maniac and are ready to pay any value to achieve it; just like Rojack who does not hesitate to kill his own wife? In Weber's observation:

> The title the novel is an ironic comment on the tenuousness of the official American dream, that hyper-conglomerate of success, salesmanship, health, and wealth which produces row on row of mannequins. Scratch the glossy surface of a contented mannequin and it bleeds a different kind of American dream, a subterranean river of untapped, ferocious, lonely and romantic desires, that concentration of ecstasy and violence which is the dream life of the nation. (2)

To conclude, it is necessary to find out whether Stephen Richard Rojack has achieved his 'American Dream' or not. And again it offers a cryptic and enigmatic elucidation. The post murder escaped life of Rojack, though, cannot satisfy the readers, the observation: "he (Mailer) presents, even prescribes, a metaphorical lesson in how to repudiate the false American Dream of materialism and position and instead to forge ahead in true American (and human) dream of courage and self-determination" (Leeds 157), is not easy to be overlooked. And it is this feature which makes Mailer's novel fascinating to read.

WORKS CITED

Adams, Laura. "Existential Battles: The Growth of Norman Mailer". Ohio: Ohio University Press, 1976.

Gutman, Stanley T. *Mankind in Barbary: The Individual and Society in the Novels of Norman Mailer*. Hanover: The University Press of New England, 1975.

Isabella, S. Joy. "Creative Versus Destructive Powers in Norman Mailer's *An American Dream*". *Language in India,* 14.9 (September 2014): 66-73. Web. 10 Feb. 2015. <www.languageinindia.com/sep2014/isabellaamericandream.pdf>

Leeds, Barry H. "Literature as life; life as literature: Mailer's existential shout of defiance in *An American Dream.*" *The Mailer Review,* 6.1 (2012): 149-57. Academic OneFile. Web. 15 Apr. 2015. <http://vlib.interchange.at/login?url=http://go.galegroup.com/ps/i.do?id=GALE%7CA3=wash89460&it=r&p=AONE&sw=w&asid=d20dbc27c81383ed9c6ob9ab58de2lb>

Mailer, Norman. *An American Dream*. London WCI: Andre Deutsch Limited, 1965.

McKinley, Maggie. "Mailer's Modern Myth: Reexamining Violence and Masculinity in *An American Dream.*" *The Mailer Review,* 6.1 (2012): 158-171. Academic OneFile. Web. 15 Apr. 2015. <http://vlib.interchange.at/login?url=http://go.galegroup.com/ps/i.do?id=GALE%7CA338575868&v=2.1&u=wash89460&it=r&p=AONE&sw=w&asid=2ded7ab816165daeb9ea7b867c79787>

Nunez, Juan Jose Torres. "Treatment of Death in Norman Mailer's *An American Dream*". *Odisea,* 4 (2003): 165-170. Web. 18 Apr. 2014.

Rajavelu, R. "Between Ideology and Murder: Fear and Power in the Twentieth Century American Fiction—A Select Study". Diss. Pondicherry University, 2006.

Weber, Brom. "A fear of dying: Norman Mailer's *An American Dream*". *Hollins Critic,* 2.3 (1965): 1-9. Academic OneFile. Web. 15 Apr. 2015. <http://vlib.interchange.at/login?url=http://go.galegroup.com/ps/i.do?id=GALE%7CA13025781&v=2.1&u=wash89460&it=r&p=AONE&sw=w&asid=b3ecabe0f2eb7d0c2228aa15a8008e2>

Zirakzadeh, Cyrus Ernesto. "Political Prophecy in Contemporary American Literature: The Left Conservative Vision of Norman Mailer" *The Review of Politics,* 69 (2007): Cambridge University Press. 625-49.

11

Howard Roark: The Mouthpiece of Ayn Rand's Philosophy of Objectivism in *The Fountainhead*

Mursalin Jahan

ABSTRACT

Ayn Rand was a Russian-American who is known in the literary circle as a novelist, philosopher, and playwright. She propounded a philosophical movement known as objectivism, which places its central emphasis on "reason, individualism, enlightened self-interest, political freedom…and the heroic vision of life's possibilities. In a nutshell, she characterized her philosophy of objectivism as "a philosophy of living on earth". Ayn Rand was an atheist who disdained altruism and propagated the virtue of selfishness to fulfill one's aspirations. Her novel *The Fountainhead* is a perfect embodiment of her doctrine of objectivity. She presents Howark Roark as an innovative protagonist who neglects traditions, confines to his own values and logical thinking, preserves the integrity of his own design and struggles against every form of social restriction. He is a strong man who ruthlessly sets his emotions aside and stays confined to his reason. He even denies his love for Dominique Francon in order to assert his individualism and self-interest. The present paper advocates the core tenets of Ayn Rand's philosophy of objectivism through Howard Roark, the protagonist of the novel *The Fountainhead*.

Keywords: Altruism, Individualism, Objectivism, Reason, Self-interest.

Ayn Rand is remembered as a fine novelist, playwright and philosopher of the twentieth-century American Literature. Ayn Rand was born on February 2, 1905 in St. Petersburg now Leningrad, Russia. After she witnessed Russian Revolution in 1917 and Civil War in 1918, she antagonized both the communist and the Tsarists. She received philosophical education in ancient philosophy especially that of Plato and Aristotle. She despised Soviet system and intended to leave Russia for United States. In New York, she became involved and influenced by the Economic journalist, Henry Hazlitt. He was a novelist, literary critic, and political philosopher. Having grown up in the totalitarian dictatorship of the Soviet Union, influenced by liberal philosophy of different intellectuals together by having fervent belief in political freedom and the right of the individual, Ayn Rand came up with a new philosophy of "living on earth" known as philosophy of objectivism. The purpose of writing *The Fountainhead* is the "projection of an ideal man" for whom she defines a rational code of ethics in the form of her philosophy of objectivism. Howard Roark, the protagonist of the novel personifies Ayn Rand's philosophy of objectivism.

She is known in literary circle as a novelist, philosopher, and playwright. Rand's view is that every novelist is a philosopher because one cannot present a picture of human existence without a philosophical framework (*Rand For New Intellectual* 5). Philosophy, Ayn Rand holds "is the science that rules men's life on earth" (Bernstein 7). Philosophy in human's life is supremely important because it guides man to the right path leading him to flourish. The values which Ayn Rand holds in her philosophy of objectivism are objective because they are derived fundamentally from facts, reality, and not from subjective whim (Bernstein 12).

Different philosophers and critics try to understand Rand's philosophy of objectivism in their own ways. She herself wrote many books unfolding her objectivist ideas. Objectivism, as a philosophical movement places its central emphasis on "reason, individualism, enlightened self-interest, political freedom...and the heroic vision of life's possibilities" (Branden "The Benefits and Hazards of the Philosophy of Ayn Rand: A Personal Statement"). Lee Penn studied the philosophy and summarizes it in his article "The Janus Face of Libertarianism Ayn Rand" as:

> At the core of Rand's philosophy was the affirmation that "A is A." This code phrase reality exists, and is objective; it is external to the human observer, and it cannot be altered by our feelings or by changing our consciousness or our perception of reality. The exercise of human reason and effort are essential to lift mankind from animal existence to a life with human dignity. (Penn 18)

Lee Penn also gives the hidden purpose behind the philosophical movement , "As the United States slouches toward bankruptcy [in culture] and despotism, Ayn Rand has offered her followers a new creed that she promised would lead them to victory over the collectivists, the parasites, and the looters" (Lee Penn "The Janus Face of Libertarianism" 18).

Ayn Rand presents Howard Roark as an innovative person who neglects traditions, confines to his own values and logical thinking, preserves the integrity of his own design and struggles against every form of social restrictions. He is a strong man who ruthlessly sets his emotions aside and stays confined to his reason. At the outset of the novel, Roark is evacuated from Stanton Institute of Technology as he is charged of "insubordination" to the administration. He condemns the traditional collectivist principles of the dean who believes that all rules of design come from great minds of their ancestors and the contemporary artist should only reproduce the traditional design. Roark disagrees with the conformist views of the dean and says that he wants to become "an architect, not an archeologist" (Rand *The Fountainhead* 22). Roark is an innovative individualist who refuses to follow the school's outdated traditions to cater to the needs of the administration of the institution.

Towards the end of the novel, Roark advocates Rand's philosophy of objectivism through a speech to deliver his plea to the jury. As a straightforward trade, Roark agrees to design Cortlandt, a housing project for Keating on the condition that the building is to be erected exactly as is designed by him. But the building is built with the blend of design of some other architects. Appalled at the amendments in the design, Roark dynamites the building one night. He argues that all special achievements have come from creators who stood opposed to the time. He explains that creativity is inextricably linked to individuals. "This creative faculty cannot be given or received, shared or borrowed. It belongs to single, individual men that which it creates is the property of the creator" (Rand *The Fountainhead* 679). He situates the government's alteration of his design within the global struggle of collectivism versus individualism and repeat Rand's idea that "good stems from independence and evil from dependence" (Burns 83).

Another theme which Roark introduces in his speech which is Rand's signature idea is the evil of altruism which is defined as "the doctrine which demands that man live for others and places others above self" (Rand *The Fountainhead* 680). The tapering of Roark's design of Cortlandt House by some men of architectural committee is a good example of altruism in the novel. The committee changes his design for the only reason that the individual, the creator does not have any right to the product of his toil. Altruists believe that the work done by a man is a public property and his rights are sacrificed to the collectives. Roark fights against such an idea by destroying his own creation on the very straightforward principle that since it is the creation of his own mind, then, he must have the right to keep the integrity of his creation. Rand identifies altruism as an evil which is reflected in the speech of Roark when he says:

> No man can live for another. He cannot share his spirit just as he cannot share his body. But the second-hander has used altruism as a weapon of exploitation and reversed the base of mankind's moral principles. Men have been taught every precept that destroys the creator. Men have been taught dependence as a virtue. The man who attempts to live for others is a dependent. He is a parasite in motive and makes parasites of those he serves.

> The relationship produces nothing but mutual corruption. It is impossible in concept. The nearest approach to it in reality—the man who lives to serve others—is the slave. If physical slavery is repulsive, how much more repulsive is the concept of servility of the spirit? The conquered slave has a vestige of honor. He has the merit of having resisted and of considering his condition evil. But the man who enslaves himself voluntarily in the name of love is the basest of creatures. He degrades the dignity of man and he degrades the conception of love. But this is the essence of altruism. (Rand *The Fountainhead* 680)

Ayn Rand intelligently concretizes the view that altruism in an evil in *The Fountainhead*. Keating rises because he is supported by Toohey, but as all parasites, falls when Toohey withdraws his support. Moreover, if the reasons of Toohey's support of Keating are sought, then they are all destructive—to make Keating who is the then leading architect under his control and to aid destroy Roark. Contrary to the popular belief that selfishness is a negative quality, Rand contends that altruism is the vicious demon trying to devour rational men (Nandakumar 2).

Roark speech also celebrates reason, another tenet of Rand's philosophy of objectivism. Ayn Rand defines and gives the importance of rationality in her book entitled *The Virtue of Selfishness*:

> Rationality is man's basic virtue, the source of all his other virtues. Man's basic vice, the source of all his evils, is the act of unfocusing his mind, the suspension of his consciousness, which is not blindness, but the refusal to see, not ignorance, but the refusal to know. Irrationality is the rejection of man's means of survival and, therefore, a commitment to a course of blind destruction; that which is anti-mind, is anti-life. The virtue of *Rationality* means the recognition and acceptance of reason as one's only source of knowledge, one's only judge of values and one's only guide to action. (Rand *The Virtue of Selfishness* 23)

Ayn Rand advocates that though man does not have any innate ideas, yet he is born with the ability to think. All human beings have a mind but only a few of them use their minds to take their independent decisions. Many people depend on authoritative figure—be their parents, teachers or others to lead their life. Roark, in both his personal and professional life, thinks independently, refuses to obey authority, reluctant to surrender the values most precious to him to the demand of others. *The Fountainhead* vindicates man's mind and supports the inflexible independence of thought. The conformist denies to use his mind, renounces himself from the responsibility of thinking and irrationally acquiescing to the ideas of others. Roark as a spokesman of Ayn Rand's philosophy of objectivism highlights the importance of reason through his trial speech:

> Man cannot survive except through his mind. He comes on earth unarmed. His brain is his only weapon. Animals obtain food by force. Man has no claws, no fangs, no horns, no great strength of muscle. He must plant his food or hunt it. To plant, he needs a process of thought. To hunt, he needs weapons, and to make weapons—a process of thought. From this simplest necessity to the highest religious abstraction, from the wheel to the skyscraper, everything we are and everything we have comes from a single attribute of man—the function of his reasoning mind.
>
> But the mind is an attribute of the individual. There is no such thing as a collective brain. There is no such thing as a collective thought. An agreement reached by a group of men is only a compromise or an average drawn upon many individual thoughts. It is a secondary consequence. The primary act—the process of reason—must be performed by each man alone. (Rand *The Fountainhead* 679)

Swayed by Roark's argument, the jury votes unanimously to acquit him. Gail Wyand hires Roark to build his building, the world's tallest skyscrapers. Thus, he achieves success on his own terms.

Ayn Rand's theory of selfishness as propagated in *The Fountainhead* is "adherence to one's own values and mind" (Bernstein 14). Andrew Bernstein discusses the theory of selfishness in his book *Objectivism in One Lesson: An Introduction to the Philosophy of Ayn Rand*:

> To be selfish, in Ayn Rand's theory, is to hold and pursue meaningful life enhancing values.... Selfishness, properly understood, involves a commitment to one's self. The deeper question, therefore, becomes: What, fundamentally, is a man's self? Ayn Rand's answer is: at one level, his values, the things he considers most important; at a deeper level, his mind—the thinking he performed in identifying and choosing those values. (13-14)

Roark perfectly acts as the mouthpiece of Ayn Rand's theory of selfishness as "adherence to once own values and mind". Roark to gets an opportunity to design the Manhattan bank building but on the condition to allow the contractor to make extraneous and inappropriate alteration to his design. Roark has to choose either an important commission with an adultered design or the maintenance of his artistic integrity (whole, pure, complete and unbroken). Though he is destitute, still he rejects the commission for the sake of maintaining the integrity of his design. When he is accused of being "fanatical and selfless" for his uncompromising stand, he is skeptical, smiles looks down at his drawing (design), moves his elbows a little pressing them to his body and says "that was the most selfish thing you've ever seen a man do" (Rand *The Fountainhead* 197). So, Roark is selfish as he is committed to himself and for him—"my work done my way"—is more important than commissions. According to Ayn Rand's sense of the term this is exactly what is called selfishness. Andrew Bernstein says that he understands that "wealth earned in this manner is a superlative good; but that money will provide him no benefit if, in the exchange, he gives up his mind, judgment, and soul, i.e., the very things that make his life and work so precious to him" (15).

Another theory which she speaks of in her philosophy of objectivism is the theory of reason. Ayn Rand advocates that though man does not have any innate ideas, yet he is born with the ability to think. All human beings have a mind, but only a few use their mind to take their independent decision. Many

people depend on authoritative figure—be it their parents, teachers or others to lead their life. Roark, in both his personal and professional life think independently, refuses to obey, reluctant to surrender the values most precious to him to the demand of others. *The Fountainhead* vindicates man's mind and supports the inflexible independence of thought. The conformist denies to use his mind, renounces himself from the responsibility of thinking and irrationally acquiescing to the ideas of others.

Roark's principles do not change over the course of the novel because a man who is ideal "the man as man should be" (Rand *The Fountainhead* 97) does not need to be changed. Despite many ups and downs in his life, he lives his life as he likes without compromising or deviating from his principles. Contrary to it, Ellsworth Toohey who always tries to influence and capture the mind and the soul of the weaker, Roark never endeavors unnecessarily to make friends and influence people. He makes friends on the basis of his reason. Dominique, brilliant and outspoken daughter of Guy Francon is convinced by Roark's idealist views. He changes the ideology of Dominique who thinks that in this rotten world greatness cannot survive. Ayn Rand argues that Keating lacks "self" as he surrenders his "self", his own independent judgment to the desires of his mother. He is passionate for painting from his childhood, but chooses to be an architect, the profession he neither likes, nor he is fit for. He gives up a career in arts not only to meet his mother's expectations who thinks that painting is a bohemian, but also to meet his mother's understanding of the expectation of the society. Thus, it can be said that Keating is a conformist and selfless. He also gives up Katie whom he loves for Dominique whom he doesn't for the very reason that he becomes an architect: to impress the people around him. By giving up his values, Keating also gives up his mind. He is no longer governed by his values, desires and knowledge but by what other think of and desire from him. His conformity and selflessness drag him to a state in which he is left without any happiness in his life and all the creative sports he possesses, have been killed. The contrast between the value of selfishness and selflessness is obvious. No matter how difficult and long the struggle of Hoark with the society is, but his life is filled with the things he loves. He has designed structures like the Aquitania Hotel and Enright House, the moments of bliss with his beloved and good time with friends such as Wynand, Mallory, Mike Konnigan, and Henry Cameron. Roark's success shows the virtue of selfishness and Keating's failure shows the evil of selflessness. Roark possesses self-esteem and is able to retain his individuality and becomes prominent in the eyes of others. He feels himself above everyone and everything else and acquiring what he desires becomes the chief aim of his life.

He is the embodiment of the philosophy of egoism of by Ayn Rand. He is self-centered and is unmindful of the whereabouts of others life. As written by Tanaji S. Kamble in her research paper entitled "Ayn Rand's Art of Characterization with Special Reference to *The Fountainhead*" that he is "an egoist who inherits nothing from others. Roark considers his life as an end in himself and not meant to any further end. As an architect, he builds to satisfy his passion for the profession"(4). He does not bother what others think of him but leads his life in a way that he neither takes care of others, nor does he want to be cared by others. He is even indifferent to the problems of Dominique whom he loves for the sake of his self-interest and self-egoism.

Howard Roark is the epitome of Ayn Rand's philosophy of objectivism, which holds that human welfare does not demand human sacrifice but it requires an independent rational mind which is the original source of all human progress and prosperity. Rand advises through her philosophy to be ready to face the consequences, whether pleasant or unpleasant but never give up reason. To embrace reason, one has to depart from emotions, faith or authoritanism as the guiding principles of life. Rand advocates that man must act for his own self-interest but not on the cost of giving up his self-respect. Altruism is an evil because it makes a person mentally and physically handicapped ultimately leading to his moral death.

WORKS CITED

Bernstein, Andrew. *Objectivism in One Lesson: An Introduction to the Philosophy of Ayn Rand*. Lanham: Hamilton Books, 2008.

Branden, Nathaniel. "The Benefits and Hazards of the Philosophy of Ayn Rand: A Personal Statement." *Association for Humanistic Psychology*, 1984. Web. 01 May 2015.

Burns, Jennifer. *Goodness of the Market: Ayn Rand and the American Right*. New York: Oxford University Press, 2009.

Kamble, S. Tanaji. "Ayn Rand's Art or Characterization with Special Reference to *The Fountainhead*." *The Criterion: An International Journal in English*, 1.3 (2010): 1-13.

Nandakumar, Renuka. "Egoism as a religion." *International Journal of Multidisciplinary Research and Development*, 2.3 (2015): 522-23. Web. 01 May 2015.

Penn, Lee. "The Janus Face of Libertarianism Ayn Rand." *SCP Journal* 35:2-35:3 n.d. Web. 01 May 2015.

Rand, Ayn. *For the New Intellectual: The Philosophy of Ayn Rand*. New York: Penguin Publication, 1961.

——. *The Fountainhead*. New York: Penguin Publication, 1993. Print.

Ryan, Scott. *Objectivism and the Corruption of Rationality: A Critique of Ayn Rand's Epistemology. New York*: Writers Club Press, 2003.

Smith, Tara. *Ayn Rand's Normative Ethics: The Virtuous Egoist Cambridge*: Cambridge University Press, 2006.

12

Oscillation between Illusion and Reality: Critiquing Salesman's Paradoxical Situation in Arthur Miller's *Death of a Salesman* and Asif Currimbhoy's *The Clock*

Lisha Sinha

ABSTRACT

Post-world war, especially the Second World War, witnessed the dawn of a new age. The war industry post-world war gained newer dimensions. Instead of producing war products, it began to manufacture goods for daily living. The society was transformed into a consumer society. The demands for newly inaugurated products like washing machine, refrigerator, iron, new cars, tires, were high. The advertisements made by the manufacturers played a major role in creating curiosity and interest in the products. At this juncture, salesman got prominence. He became the epitome of success, happiness and luxury which in turn represented the American Dream. On the other side, the scenario of the postcolonial India was different. Unlike America, which became a land of promises post-world war, India became land of chaos post-independence. By this time, the American dream was a global phenomenon, but it hit hard on the lives of the natives of India. After the initial flag independence, the elite class rushed to take the vacant position of the colonisers. As a result, the

country was neo-colonised at the hands of the new dominants that were largely capitalist in nature. The salesman at this point of time was disillusioned as they faced the harsh reality of the world sales. The following paper will attempt to discuss that how the plays like Arthur Miller's *Death of a Salesman* (1949) and Asif Currimbhoy's *The Clock* (1956) played a crucial role in bringing out the actual condition of salesman who oscillates between illusion and reality. The paper will also focus to bring out the paradoxical situation of a salesman in the technological society.

Keywords: Salesman, Illusion, Reality, American dream, *The Clock*.

In the contemporary scenario, the societal status of any individual is measured by money and power. Money and power has become key element to path of success. Money, power, and success are actually the essence of American dream. Post-world war, especially the Second World War, America witnessed the dawn of a new age. Instead of producing war products, the war industry began to manufacture goods for daily living. The society was transformed into a consumer society. At this juncture, America became a land of opportunity. It became a field of success where anyone could dream to be prosperous even if the person was penniless. The society gradually shifted its focus from agricultural and manufacturing industries. The society began to favour the white collar jobs and so there was a great deal of consumption as well as production. The demands for newly inaugurated products like washing machine, refrigerator, iron, new cars, tires, branded liquors, designer dresses like nylon stockings were high. The advertisements made by the manufacturers played a major role in creating curiosity and interest in the products. At this juncture, salesman got prominence. The salesman with a note of positivity and confidence became the icon of the modern society. He became the epitome of success, happiness and luxury which in turn represented the American dream. The American dream became a kind of dream which will soon come true if accompanied with

high desires and hard work. On the other side, the scenario of the postcolonial India was different. Unlike America, which became a land of promises post-world war, India became land of chaos post-independence. By this time, the American dream was a global phenomenon, but it hit hard on the lives of the natives of India. After the initial flag independence, the elite class rushed to take the vacant position of the colonisers. As a result, the country was neo-colonised at the hands of the new dominants that were largely capitalist in nature. Initially, the promises made by the capitalist dream soon lead the individuals into isolation, family disintegration and finally disillusion. At this point of time, the plays like Arthur Miller's *Death of a Salesman* (1949) and Asif Currimbhoy's *The Clock* (1956) played a crucial role in bringing out the actual condition of salesman who oscillates between illusion and reality. The plays attempt to bring out the paradoxical situation of salesman in the technological society. This is perhaps demonstrated better by salesman Willy Loman, the protagonist of *Death of a Salesman* and Henry, the protagonist of *The Clock*.

Miller keeps Willy Loman, the salesman, unaware of the true nature of the capitalist society disguised in the veil of American dream and thus is left unrealized until his death. One can notice that Willy has absorbed the societal values of the materialistic world. The 'tomorrow' has a greater significance for Willy because the hopes of future keeps him escaping from the harder facts of truth that job of a salesman is one of the toughest ways to gain money and power. He feels that, "...what could be more satisfying than to be able to...pick up a phone and be remembered and loved and helped by so many people" (p. 58). Willy fails to realize that he is only a medium between the consumers and producers. He also does not understand that the world of sales run on the wheels of profit. The moment one fails to satisfy his consumer and producer, he will have no place in the money-making society. And that people cared only about goods and products becomes clear when none of the people turns around for the funeral of once 'high esteemed' Willy Loman. The people who used to display lots of affection and concern ultimately prove only as buyers and sellers leaving Willy

to die in his dreams. But unlike Miller, Currimbhoy has carefully chosen his protagonist Henry in *The Clock* who chooses to live amidst the crude reality of the world. For Willy, only the world of success attracted, but the same world repelled Henry. "All I want out of life is the right to live as I choose.... Somehow it's always been a fight because I happened to be the underdog every time...and now I am tired" (p. 17). Henry seems to realize the self-centred nature of the capitalist world which has gained newer dimensions post-independence. Henry knows that such world is full of dominance and false promises. The job of salesman has denied Henry the feeling of a free individual. He is tired of false appreciations and recognition. On his way of creating false dreams for others, his own life has become monotonous and futile. He seeks to free himself from the illusory world to lead his own way of life.

Unlike Henry, Willy Loman has his spirits fully charged. He still thinks that he can make his way through the white-collar society and gain rightful position in the society. From the very beginning, Willy has inculcated his own pursuits of dream within his children. This in turn has done no good. Instead of encouraging his children to pursue better studies, he encouraged them to focus on their physique which is essential in the world of sales. Willy is ignorant that a good physique may give a good impression in the trade market but for a stable future, education and experience matters for long time success. And his friend Charley's son Bernard serves as the perfect example of success. The failures of children represent the failure of American dream about which Willy is completely ignored. The ignorance is another illusive nature of American dream as it keeps a person moving forward and makes people like Willy Loman feels that "I will never get behind a wheel the rest of my life" (p. 52). For Willy, the life is full of possibilities. But for Henry possibilities have become obsolete. His experience in the trade field thrushes him with a harsher reality that dream never exists. They are socially constructed with an aim to subvert and exploit the labour of the individual in order to fill the pockets of the beneficiaries. The sly approaches of concern from the money makers are only another sign of making profit. This becomes clearer when Henry's boss approaches Henry and expresses his vicious desires for his secretary Jean. The boss wants to favour Henry in exchange of Jean. The disillusioned Henry is well aware of illusive promises. He rightfully expresses, "Yes I know, right down from the General Manager to humble little office boy, we must all sell, sell, and sell" (p. 41).

However, salesman like Willy Loman has succumbed himself to the false advertisements of the materialistic world. He considered himself as a salesman who in Miller's words as mentioned in *Salesman in Beijing* is "vital force in building the trade and commercial network of the country" (p. 130). The illusion lies in the fact that in the trade of sales the importance of a salesman lies only to the point of making profit. The moment he stops profiting the company, he is thrown away just like "eat the orange and throw the peel away" (p. 58). Willy seems to have mixed the personal relations with business. He is unaware that the capitalist world has no place for relationships. Howard fires Willy out of the job because he feels that the old man is no longer a 'vital force' for his company profits. Even here, we can find Willy unable to realise the harsh reality of the American dream. Willy is baffled to the extent that he cannot even understand that there is no space for kinships in the world of sales. On the other hand, Henry is clearly aware about the money-minded industry. He moves ahead of Willy in respect of gaining own dignity by resigning his job before he is fired by his boss. Unlike Willy, he refuses to be a victim of intrusive commercialism. His dream of prosperity is shattered because the commercial market has slowly invaded its way into his daily life and moral values. He is forced to do things which are beyond his own expectations. His own self-image is hurt when he is asked by his boss to fire an employee because he has failed to achieve the target sales. At this point, Henry seems to have realized his own unstable position in the world of sales and thus is thoroughly disillusioned with the capitalist society, "Do you know I was told the other day by the boss to fire one of my boys merely because he had failed to keep pace with others and sold less" (p. 16). The deadlines and quotas are nuisance for Henry unlike Willy who aspires to get his commission from his sales to fulfil his dreams of living the standards of the society. Willy is a slave to the materialistic world. His ignorance brings disintegration within his own family. For Willy, a man with confidence and positivity can achieve success. This is what he teaches his children too. But in reality, the failures of securing essential educational qualifications have failed his sons to achieve success. This crude reality has become an intruder to Willy's dreams. He has shut himself against all the truths and believes that his children will be soon starting a grand business in the West. Willy Loman "... is a man who wishes his reality to come into line with his hopes, a man desperate to have his mask on the world through his own endeavour and through those of his children" (Bigsby 101).

Willy Loman lives in a Utopian land of new identity and new hopes. His illicit relation with another woman reflects his extreme zeal to success. The woman with whom he has an affair is the secretary of the office where he trades his sales. His affair is not a breach of trust with his wife Linda but rather an attempt to achieve a high sales target. But in the process of his money making, he loses the confidence of his son Biff and later himself. Willy's attempt to secure 'Happy Family', a feature of American dream, proves to be an illusion. But unfortunately, Willy fails to realise the broken status of his family. He still feels that Biff is the future of glory and fame for Willy. Willy's confident nature as a salesman persists even though he is now a failed salesman, a failed husband and most importantly, a failed father. *Death of a Salesman* "...concerns the Loman family. Willy is a failed salesman where sons Biff and Happy are also failures.... The Great American Dream is embodied in Willy's brother Ben who went into the jungle at 18 and came out rich at 21 and appears to Willy from time to time in the play" (Selden 57). Ben in the play symbolises the American dream that Willy Loman aspires for. Willy fails to understand the actual situation of Ben. He also fails to realise that Ben's becoming rich is no short-cut process. It needs long enduring moments irrespective of charming and attractive physique.

Henry unlike Willy stands very clear when it comes to distinguish between illusion and reality. He is aware that money and power causes happiness only at the superficial level. In actual scenario, living one's own way of life is more important. His twenty years of salesmanship has choked him. Unlike Willy, Henry's choice of becoming salesman is a forceful choice against his will. At an early age, he drops his college to bear the responsibility of his pregnant girlfriend. And since a salesman job requires a minimum educational qualification, Henry sought refuge to selling. From the very beginning, he faced the harsh truth that materialistic world acts like a slow poison in the life of salesman who has to struggle everyday to reach the target sales. The worst affected is his family. He has no sense of concern towards his nagging wife as well as his children. His main motto of life unlike Willy is to escape from all his responsibilities and undone his mistakes committed in his past, "[He leans out of the window and looks at the sky]...look out, look yonder. There is always a little window in the prison of life. And it looks into a wider world and into an infinite heaven. Nothing filthy up there. I could sit and watch the stars all my life...and be happy..." (p. 18). Interestingly, on one side Henry seeks to be alone but on the other favours the company of Jean with whom he senses a feeling of freedom. Willy had an affair with woman because he dreamt of creating more sales. But Henry's affair with secretary of the office is not to gain favours from his boss. His sole purpose is to get wayward from his daily monotonous routine.

Willy Loman's life gropes towards the way of a dream which in reality never comes true. In his life of selling goods, he himself has become a slave to the consumer society. Even though Willy has burden of making mortgage payments, he still seeks to upgrade his status by consuming goods required to live by the standards of society. Things are opposite for Henry. He does not even care to celebrate his birthday because he refuses to bend down to the world of materialism. Birthday celebrations are special mechanisms of capitalist society to sell consumer goods and earn money. Henry refuses to trap himself further against the fancy notions of the materialistic world. Throughout the play, Henry acts as an antagonist to the dreams of success. On the other hand, Willy even at his old age seeks to earn his living. He becomes a dreamer and loves to exaggerate his target sales from past 1928 to keep him away from present reality. He never realizes that he is ruled by his illusive thoughts which his son Biff clearly realizes, "The man don't know who we are!... We never told the truth for ten minutes in the house" (p. 97). Illusion has subverted reality to such extent that "Willy exists in a world that increasingly detaches itself from him, reminding him daily of his own insignificance" (Roudane 80). Willy gradually distances from reality and this becomes evident with his habit of talking to himself. The conversations are mainly related to the past. This shows that he is unable to accept today's reality and has blurred him to illusion. His illusory belief or American dream is exampled best when he has a 'private conversation' with his brother Ben. Henry on the other side is facing the harsh truth that the market of sales takes blood out of the soul irrespective of personal loss and mental peace. And despite the fact that his resigning the job will bring the family financially crushed, he sticks to his decision of not going back to the world that offers fake promises of success in exchange of sense of isolation and displacement.

Willy lives in the world of past. It has frozen him to the time from where he never attempts to come out. He believes only in the world of sales which includes even selling himself. His death was not an escape from reality but another futile attempt to comply with his American dream. On the other Henry seeks death not to fulfil his dream to success but to escape from the competitive world of sales. Willy Loman and Henry are Janus faced and complement each other. Willy represents the illusion and Henry symbolises the reality of the world of Capitalism, which comes in disguise of American Dream and Post-colonial Dream. In any ways, death of a salesman occurs slowly and steadily after the 'tick-tock' of the clock covers miles before reaching the ultimate sale and purchase.

WORKS CITED

Bigsby, Christopher. *Arthur Miller: A Critical Study*. Cambridge: Cambridge University Press, 2005.

Currimbhoy, Asif. *The Clock*. Calcutta: Writer's Workshop, 1993.

Miller, Arthur. *Salesman in Beijing*. New York: Viking Adult, 1984.

Miller, Arthur. *The Death of a Salesman*. New York: Viking Press, 1973.

Roudane C. Matthew. "*Death of a Salesman* and the poetics of Arthur Miller". *The Cambridge Companion to Arthur Miller*, Ed. Christopher Bigsby. Cambridge: Cambridge University Press, 1997.

13

Abigail's Witchcraft in Arthur Miller's *The Crucible*: A Feminist Approach

Amna Shamim

ABSTRACT

Feminist theories have long been involved in interpreting androtexts. There has, indeed, been a vast difference in the portrayal of women by male and female writers. In twentieth-century American Literature, male writers like Edward Albee, Eugene O'Neil, Tennessee Williams, Sam Shepard, Langston Hughes, T.S. Eliot and Neil Simon projected women characters in diverse lights. Arthur Miller's works are similar in some ways, but different from these playwrights in the larger perspective. This paper reflects on Miller's treatment of women both in the traditional and non-traditional aspects in his play *The Crucible*. The work shows women practising witchcraft and dealing in devilish tasks. This paper also studies the varied approaches of Miller towards women that have been represented through *The Crucible*.

Keywords: Feminism, Arthur Miller, Women, Witchcraft, Drama.

Feminism in the twentieth century came up with a definition that was different from the 'prudish approach' of the Victorian era. It was marked by the advent of more freedom and rights of women that were not bestowed upon the gender till the nineteenth century. It took decades for women to reach upto the level in society where they could demand their rights and think of themselves, other than thinking only of their male counterparts. Women in the Jazz Age were termed as "Progressive Women" as they could oust out of the social constraints that were imposed on them and do all that was earlier considered the domain of men. Progressive women could take up a job, smoke, dance in public, or wear short skirts. Other than these practices that women took up during the era that later became a topic of debate, they became a major part of the workforce. The kind of work given to them then was categorized as "women's work" and they were only entrusted with works like teaching, nursing, and answering calls for companies. That was also the time when women's salaries were not equal to the salaries of men. At the same job and position, women were considered inferior. Male chauvinism persisted among the males who could not endure the sight of women working alongside them and becoming independent as that was likely to broaden their mindset and challenge the years-old patriarchal tradition.

Considering women as important and giving them equal role in life and literature was, especially for male writers, a sacrilege way back in the nineteenth and twentieth centuries. Arthur Miller did not follow the league and projected his female characters as important and powerful. When women were shown as fragile beings, they were given the role of the backbone of the male community, and when they were portrayed as strong individuals, they were shown to be capable enough to mould the story or situations according to their wish. The female characters in *The Crucible* (1953) are ahead of their times. In a society where women were expected to be obedient and submissive, young girls like Abigail and Mercy Lewis move out of their cubby spaces to achieve their means. They do not fear the consequences of being caught and tagged as a witch but do things to satisfy their desires.

The works in those days were malecentric and laid less focus upon the wishes and desires of the female race. Women were stuck in the jeopardy of being objectified and self-objectification. They were taught to be obedient and repressive because they were expected to satisfy the carnal desires of the males without paying heed to their own preferences. Studies reveal that female desire is stronger than male desire and that men suppress these desires in order to maintain their hegemony. Baumeister and Tweng studied the sexual instincts of the females and stated their findings in their research paper entitled "Cultural Suppression of Female Sexuality":

> The double standard of sexual morality has condemned certain sexual activities by women while permitting the identical actions for men (166). A similar line of argument holds that the suppression of female sexuality frees men from having to satisfy the huge female demand for sex, which otherwise would make men feel burdened or insecure (169). Men have conspired to set up a system that oppresses women so as to stifle female sexuality and that men benefit from that stifling. (170)

The double standards of society are predominantly felt by both male and female writers. These standards were not talked of till twentieth century when feminist critiques and gynocritics took the literary world by storm. Women had a closer brush with reality in the context of female suppression, so they could bring out that trauma on the pages more aptly than their male counterparts. Victorian Age saw many writers who portrayed women as insane, trying to keep out a justified outlook towards the females of those times. These individuals were not considered worthy of taking any kind of decisions and were treated as commodities for sexual gratification. The fear of the consequences of giving vent to female sexuality is evidently seen in works by male writers. One such writer is Bram Stoker who develops the characters of Mina and Lucy in *Dracula*. These women are eyed by the Dracula who plans to turn them into vampires and by doing so release their carnal desires. The novel shows that women, as evil, are in a position to subdue men and gain an extra edge over them. D.H. Lawrence's controversial novel, *Lady Chatterley's Lover*, deals with the same issue of female sexuality in a derogatory manner. A woman's desires are shown as a means for her to find release. And through this, the writers justify the suppression of females and female sexuality.

Lolita complex in *The Crucible* can be seen through the relationship of Abigail Williams and John Proctor. Abigail, a seventeen-year old girl, develops an illicit relationship with John Proctor, who is sixty-five and finds it hard to come out of the trance. The story reveals that these two are together for some time and enjoy each other's company to the extent that John Proctor distances himself from his wife. But the puritan ideology would not have accepted such philanderers in their midst. This relationship does not take long to prick John Proctor's conscience, and his guilt of cheating on his wife leads him back to Elizabeth Proctor. Abigail feels dejected and in order to have him solely to herself, she becomes jealous of Elizabeth on whom she later performs witchcraft.

American society believed in and feared witchcraft. There are instances from real life situations also that point towards this practice in the nineteenth and twentieth centuries. Out of many trials and persecutions witnessed by the people of America, the Salem witch trials of 1692 are remembered till date because of the series of hangings ordered during those trials of the common people. Initially, the focus of such acts, too, was only on the elite section of society. Many people were hanged during the Salem trials, most of them being women.These trials came to be called by people as mass murders, mass hysteria and mass executions. All these instances were captured by literary scholars in their works. Other than Miller, Esther Forbes' wrote *A Mirror for Witches* in 1928 which also took up the Salem witch trials as its central theme. The story is about a girl named Doll Bilby who is deserted by her relatives on the charges of being a witch. Later she is called in court during the Salem witch trials. Women like Esther Forbes and Marion Starkey (*The Devil in Massachussets*, 1949) had already touched the trials of Salem when Arthur Miller came up with his play. Miller tried to make his play real—like by using the names of actual people involved in the trials—Tituba, Abigail Williams, Samuel Parris, Betty Parris, Rebecca Nurse and Putnams.

Abigail is seen as a strong and bold woman who does not shy away from doing devilish acts even in the times when people were punished for such deeds. Not only does she herself gets involved in witchcraft but also she cajoles other girls to accompany her and become a part and parcel of her plans. She is also shown to be decisive and ruthless in her approach towards her works. On getting scared, Mary Warren tries to rescue herself out of the situation but she is pulled in again by Abigail:

> Mary Warren: I never done none of it, Abby. I only looked!
>
> Mercy, *moving menacingly toward Mary*: Oh, you're a great one for lookin', aren't you, Mary Warren? What a grand peeping courage you have! (*The Crucible* 19 emphasis in original)

The women are depicted as practicing devilish acts in order to achieve their means. *The Crucible* projects women in the society with either good or bad characteristics. The play adheres to the tenets of the then American society that judged people on the basis of black and white, not open to the idea of people possessing grey shades. Abigail Williams is the antagonist who performs witchcraft and is not even sympathetic towards the Reverend who brought her up. On the contrary, Elizabeth is a virtuous and morally upright women who is cold and meek, although she could not stand the sight of Abigail the moment she realizes that she and her husband are into a relationship. The morality and chastity of a woman was considered to be the best characteristic of women and only such women were looked at with respect and considered "good". Abigail's character is dark and gloomy who is deprived of parental love and has gone through difficult times. She could have been shattered because of the status that she had in society but she manages to keep herself together and does not accept anybody and everybody's commands. This is evident in the play where she replies to Reverend Parris' questioning of her work status, "They want slaves, not such as I. Let them send to Barbados for that. I will not black my face for any of them!" (*The Crucible* 12).

The reason for the barbaric acts of Abigail, both devilish and selfish, can be traced back to her childhood. She is an orphan who is taken up by her uncle, Reverend Parris. He looks after her and has genuine concern for her. But Abigail's heart is wretched and full of pain due to the adverse circumstances that she has been caught into. This repressed pain leads her into having a relationship with John Proctor whom she misunderstands and falls prey to his sweet talks. When even he distances himself from her, she goes into a hysterical state in which she commits abominated acts. Psychologists study such real-life traumas through the Objectification Theory which states that the mental health of a female is somehow related to the Sexual Objectification of that female that disproportionately affects her, leading to depression, sexual dysfunction or/and hysteria. Psychologists from the Department of Psychology, University of Tennessee came up with the interpretation of some scholars who, by and large, pointed towards the events occurring in the life of females during childhood or later that lead to their inappropriate behaviour. It can be substantiated with the help of these interpretations:

> Oppressive events or living in an environment that is filled with such stimuli have been theorized to be risk factors for substance abuse problems (Zucker and Landry, 2007). Clark et al. (1999) postulated that individuals who deal with oppressive events may have feelings of anger and depression, which may then lead to coping via use of alcohol or other substances to manage these feelings. Furthermore, Zucker and Landry (2007) posited that women may cope with experiences of sexism by using substances as a numbing mechanism. Relatedly, Jacobson (1986) postulated that women may smoke, and perhaps use other substances, to cope with being undervalued and under-paid and because they fear that if they express their feelings they will come off as unfeminine. (Szymanski 18)

The act of witchcraft worked as a "numbing mechanism" for Abigail. She found an outlet and a means to gratify her instincts and desires. Witchcraft gave women what men intentionally hid from them—"power"; the power to control and be the possessor of things and others' life. Men had been enjoying the privilege of being the chief and heads of the families wherein they could order, scold or even beat people who were supposed to be under their guardianship. Yet, history reveals that men's demand for power is unquenching thirst and this is the reason that they were also found guilty of practicing the art of black magic. Louise Jackson discusses the same in her work on women's confessions of witchcraft in the seventeenth century:

> [W]itch-hunting was woman-hunting—a way of sifting out subversive females—but that the women accused, in their confessions, were judging themselves in their role as neighbours, wives and mothers. Indeed it seems to be the case that some accused witches were, within their court confessions, contextualising their own insecurities and experiences within the linguistic framework of demonology. (64)

Other female characters in the play, Tituba, Mrs. Ann Putnam, Mercy Lewis, Mary Warren, Rebecca Nurse and Elizabeth Porter are either power-hungry females or subservient and obedient wives. The play strangely leaves one gasping on Elizabeth's confession of being cold towards her husband that led him to go astray. Women are shown as either sturdy individuals who consider it their moral obligation to look after and keep their husbands happy, or they belong to the category of witches who curse, abuse and cast spells. In both the forms, Miller's women in *The Crucible* belong to the changing times and try by all means to fit in the new mould and bring a revolutionary change in the role and status of women in the prudish and snobbish American society.

WORKS CITED

Baumeister, Roy F. and Jean M. Twenge. "Cultural Suppression of Female Sexuality". *Review of General Psychology*, 6.2 (2002): 166-203.

Bigsby, Christopher. *Arthur Miller: A Critical Study*. New York: Cambridge University Press, 2005.

Bomarito, Jessica, and Jeffrey W. Hunter, eds. *Feminism in Literature: A Gale Critical Companion*. Thomson Gale, Vol. 4, 2005.

Clark, R. et al. "Racism as a Stressor for African Americans: A Biopsychosocial Model". *American Psychologist*, 54 (1999): 805-816.

Jackson, Louise. "Witches, Wives and Mothers: Witchcraft Persecution and Women's Confessions in Seventeenth-Century England". *Women's History Review*, 4.1 (1995): 63-84.

Jacobson, B. *Beating the Ladykillers: Women and Smoking*. London: Pluto Press, 1986.

Lawrence, D.H. *Lady Chatterley's Lover*. Project Gutenberg, Australia, 2001. Web. 8 May 2015.

Miller, Arthur. *The Crucible*. New York: Penguin, 1996.

Stoker, Bram. *Dracula*. The Online Literary Library, n.pag., Web. 8 May 2015.

Schroeder, Patricia R. "American Drama, Feminist Discourse, and Dramatic Form: In Defense of Critical Pluralism". *Journal of Dramatic Theory and Criticism*, Spring 1993: 103-18.

Szymanski, Dawn M. et al. "Sexual Objectification of Women: Advances to Theory and Research". *The Counselling Psychologist*, 39.1 (2011): 6-38.

Zucker, A.N. and L.J. Landry. "Embodied Discrimination: The Relation of Sexism and Distress to Women's Drinking and Smoking Behaviours." *Sex Roles*, 56 (2007): 193-203.

14

Thom Gunn: The American Phase

Naila Ahmad Suhail

ABSTRACT

Thom Gunn, a colossal poetic figure in mid-twentieth century American poetry, is a bundle of contradictions: the quintessential San Franciscan who held a British passport, a Romatic who was entranced by classical control, an experimentalist who never renounced rhyme and meter and an anti-authoritarian populist with mandarin standards. The present paper seeks to dwell upon Gunn's existentialist quest in his poems. His status as a survivor is apparent in his poem "In the Post Office" where he admits that he is "recording so that I may later read/ of what has happened, whether between sheets/ or in post offices or on the streets".

Gunn's favourite definition of poetry is "memorable speech". His nine published volumes of poetry show a continuous thematic and stylistic opening out from his earlier introspective poems of separateness, violence and imposition of will (Fighting Terms), to the later phase in which he wrote poems on nihilism (*From the Highest Camp*), drug culture (*Moly*) and homosexuality (*Jack Staws Castle*).

Ironically, Gunn's greatest moment as a poet came at his most difficult time—the AIDS epidemic that devastated San Francisco. In one month alone, he lost four close friends. Out of this personal and public crisis grew his next collection *The Man with Night Sweats* (1992), which contains the finest gay elegies ever written and will probably stand as the central poetic testament of those plague years.

His particular genius has been to embody the human and artistic contradictions of his age not only as a poet but also as a perceptive critic of gay poetry.

Keywords: Existentialist quest, nihilism, drug-culture, homosexuality, gay elegies, violence.

Thomson William Gunn, a colossal poetic figure in mid-twentieth century American poetry, is a bundle of contradictions: the quintessential San Franciscan who held a British passport, a Romantic who was entranced by classical control, an experimentalist who never renounced rhyme and meter and an anti-authoritarian populist with mandarin standards.

Gunn's poems show not just an honest account of the self but a genuine attempt at understanding the intellectual's conditions in modern life. He is, undoubtedly, one of the greatest poets writing in English after the forties. Though the group, 'The Movement', to which he initially belonged, got disbanded in the 1960s, Gunn continued to share the belief of the Movement poets that poetry should be well made and craftsman-like, utilizing traditional rhythms and rhyme-schemes. Like other Movement poets (Philip Larkin, Donald Davie, Elizabeth Jennings, Robert Conquest, John Wain, Kingsley Amis and D.J. Enright) he was anti-phoney, robust, sceptical, and ironical.

While still an undergraduate, Gunn met Mike Kitay, an American, who was to become the leading influence on his life, and consequently, on his poetry. After leaving Cambridge, he followed Kitay to the United States, something made possible by the award of a creative writing fellowship at Stanford University, where he became a student of the poet and critic, Yvor Winters. Except for the occasional visit, and one year-long sojourn in the mid-60s, Gunn was never to return to England. He had decided to make America his home, and settled in San Francisco in 1960.

Nine major collections of Gunn's poetry have appeared since he began writing in 1951. They are *Fighting Terms* (1953), *The Sense of Movement* (1957), *My Sad Captains* (1961), *Touch* (1967), *Moly* (1971), *Jack Straw's Castle* (1976), *The Passages of Joy* (1982), *The Man with Night Sweats* (1992), and, most recently, *Boss Cupid* (2000). Gunn's favourite definition of poetry is "memorable speech". Many of his poems expressed fairly complex ideas with intricately extended metaphors, a style which helped him earn the label of a 'Modern Metaphysical Poet'. During the '70s and '80s, when he started to write out of his experiences as a user of soft and hard drugs, and to write more openly of his life as a homosexual, there were a number of critics who felt that he was squandering his talent, indulging in what one called 'hippy silliness', or abandoning himself to what another called 'vacant counter-cultural slovenliness' (htpp://poetry.about.com/b/a082207.htm). However, the majority of his readers agreed with Hugh Haughton's comment that "Gunn, though strangely neglected in England, is one of the most singular and compelling poets in English during the past half-century" (htpp://britannica.com-article). His status as a survivor is apparent in his poem "*In the Post Office*" where he admits that he is "recording so that I may later read/ of what has happened, whether between sheets/ or in post offices or on the streets".

Gunn was quite consciously a writer of contrasts, who drew on a wide range of influences and modes. According to Sean O' Brien, Gunn's work illustrates with unusual clarity some of the debates poetry in English has pursued this century—form versus improvisation, diction versus talk, the American way versus the English tradition, even, at times, authenticity versus art. To contain these contradictory impulses and, over the past 40 years, to have generated a body of work which anybody wanting to understand the period and identify some of its best poems will find essential reading—this is quite an achievement. Gunn's favoured definition of poetry is "memorable speech". He has certainly provided his share (quoted in Ramanan 1989: 186).

Gunn's poetry is characterized by a cool sense of intellectual detachment and a penetratingly lucid ability to follow experience to its resolvable core. This sensibility is offered in disarmingly casual, laid-back tones inherited from the post-60s American poetry. Gunn admitted that "Spoken word has always been important for poetry, and I've always acted on the assumption, probably due to my earlier education, that poetry is metrically heard as much as read" (Gunn 1982: 176). He successfully pulled off that rare and necessary trick of reinventing himself through American Poetry, thus bypassing the pedestrianism which blighted so many of his British contemporaries. This ongoing reinvention and self-resurrection is one of the most interesting and inspiring subtexts of his *Collected Poems*. Thus, to Gunn, the writing of poetry is a 'technique' of comprehension involving the full use of rational power and moral judgement. He insists that if the process of poetry is exploration or adventure, then its goal is understanding. He is essentially a philosophical poet, addressing himself to perennial questions of love, identity, freedom and choice but finding his answers in the immediate present. His achievements over the four decades of writing are those of an innovator pushing the boundaries of the accepted subject-matter of poetry. He is a master of the compressed lyric executed in formal stanzas, but he is always modern and he is also compellingly truthful.

The American phase of Gunn's writing began with his migration to America in 1954. *The Sense of Movement* written while teaching at Stanford University is generally considered to be his self-portrait. It impressively highlights the poet's obsessive interest in the will.

"On the Move", the first poem in this volume, is his most famous piece and among the best-known of all post-war poems. It has Sartre's theory of existentialism as its base. The implication is that man is irrevocably linked to humanity and his individual freedom rests on the freedom of others. The poem features young motor cyclists roaring away 'in goggles' and 'gleaming jackets' trophied with dust. "They are emblems of large human conditions", according to G.S. Fraser, "and are not riding towards any known goal but as fast as possible away from a known and frustrating background" (Dyson 1990: 21). The question arises whether they are in search of an identity or have consciously "chosen to lose their individuality" (Bold 1969: 26).

"Silver Age" is one of the few poems of Gunn, which clearly represents 'Movement' Poetry as it depicts a clash between conflicting attitudes and values and shows a cynical irreverence for the past. It introduces Centurion in the first stanza who is sitting drowsily in a corner "with his head gentle over/ The swelling breast plate." Asking him where true Rome is found would not yield any results as he would just guide the person through the moonlight of modernity, without reaching any satisfactory destination. This is because the Centurion is ignorant about Rome's past, where its true spirit lay. It is a period which now lies in 'darkness'. Nonetheless, the Centurion takes confident steps towards this 'river of darkness'.

> ...a river never crossed
> By any but some few who hate the moonlight.

The Centurion grips the poet 'like a cold strap of leather' while leading him. The irony is that he detests modernity or 'moonlight' but has to live his life in it while yearning for the darkness of the past. The imagery consists of the all-pervading atmosphere of darkness contrasted with the criss-crossing moonlight. The words are simple but the theme is fraught with multiple meanings.

"The Allegory of the Wolf Boy" has been termed by various critics as the finest poem of *The Sense of Movement.* It is an allegory of human nature depicting the basic duality in man's nature wherein both human and animal instincts co-exist. Alan Bold calls it "a sustained image of civilized English life acting like a vicious trap to squeeze all impulse and instinct out of the individual" (Bold 1976: 86). This poem features the transformation of a boy into an animal because he identifies himself with it. This boy is like any other normal child in appearance and behaviour during the day but when night approaches, he feels compelled, by his basic instincts, to break away from stifling social conventions, shed his clothes, assume an animal form and veer into the 'darkness'. However, his effort is futile because he can never really escape from the confines of his background. His 'bleeding paws' become symbols of his anguish. The poem consists of four stanzas of six lines and abounds in modern and very graphic images probably inspired by Keat's "Ode to Autumn".

Gunn's third collection of poems, *My Sad Captains* (1961), has twenty-nine poems and is divided into two phases, out of which sixteen poems, which make the first part, are written in metrical style whereas the concluding thirteen poems are written in syllabics and have looser rhythms and forms. Writing about this division to Fabers & Fabers in 1972, Gunn has said:

> In 1961, I published *My Sad Captains* which is in two parts. The first-half is a culmination of my old style—metrical, rational but may be starting to get a little more humane. The second half consists of taking up of that humaner impulse in a series of syllabic poems which were something new in my work.

Experiments with free verse became increasingly obvious in Gunn's work from the 1960s. The discipline of writing to a specific set of visual images coupled with the liberation of free verse constituted a new source of rule and energy in his poems. This major stylistic change in his work was combined with the other changes in his life—his taking up permanent residence in America, from academic Cambridge to bohemian San Francisco, his becoming openly gay, his drug taking, his writing about the 'urban underbelly'—caused many to conjecture how his lifestyle was affecting his work.

"In Santa Maria de Popolo", acclaimed as the best poem of this collection, is a beautifully written piece based on nihilism. It deals with the close inspection of a painting which hangs in a chapel and is viewed by the poet piece by piece as the first rays of the morning sun fall on it and gradually cover it. It shows a man who has fallen off his horse, sprawled on the ground with out-flung arms facing blinding light in a state of stupor. The poet realizes that the painting portrays the story of the sinner Saul who had undergone a great transformation when confronted by divine light and had become the great apostle Paul.

> .... I see him sprawl,
> Foreshortened from the head, with hidden face,
> Where he had fallen, Saul becomes Paul.

However, though the poet watches the painting carefully, he is not enlightened by it and does not understand its subject:

> What is it you mean
> In the wide gesture of lifting arms.

Subsequently, he moves into a church and sees a congregation, consisting mostly of old ladies kneeling in reverence with their frail hands folded. The poet contrasts this scene with the painting and says that the poor arms of these old people are already too tired to equal the renewed vitality of Paul who had his arms flung out. The poem consists of four stanzas of eight lines each and has been unanimously praised by various critics. Yvor Winters echoed the popular sentiment when he not only admired its command on grammar and syntax but also called it

> remarkably vigorous; it is far better than anything by half a dozen poets of this century who are commonly called great.... Like many of Gunn's poems, it exists on the narrow line between great writing and skilful journalism. (Extract from section on 'Early Gunn': 1967)

"From the Highest Camp", one of the most accomplished poems in the entire range of Gunn's poetry, has the dual theme of endurance in the face of extreme circumstances and nihilism or nothingness, embedded in it. It is an allegory not only in respect of its theme but also in its message. The setting of the poem is a desolate place high up in the mountains where everything is so frozen, static and purposeless that it seems like "the last camp of experience." If one has to save himself from extinction, he must be prepared to bear the harshest condition of existence. This metaphysical idea of nihilism is a substantial facet of experience for Thom Gunn, which he feels every man has to come to terms with at some point in his life. It is a short poem of two stanzas with an irregular rhyme-pattern.

Gunn's early poems displayed a blind admiration for toughness but he gradually learnt to distinguish between the action of the tough and their toughness. The poem "Innocence" has a young man from the Nazi youth corps of the 1940s as its main protagonist and explores the darker side of the qualities of toughness that contribute to making him a perfect soldier but a deficient human being. He exists in an attitude of 'compact innocence' wherein he has qualities like courage, endurance, loyalty and skill but he is, at the same time, ignorant of all finer feelings of sensitivity, sympathy and compassion. In short, he is a 'hardened instrument', devoid of conscience.

"Considering the Snail" is a poem highlighting Gunn's attitudinal change from a fascination with tough irrational ways to absorption with the seemingly insignificant quiet progression symbolized by a snail's movement. The snail is a creature with no identity and goes unnoticed in the rain-darkened earth. However, to Gunn, its movement is neither aimless nor futile but exhibits its 'strong will' and 'concentrated energy'. Its single-minded determination to pursue its path is imaginatively depicted by the poet in the following lines:

> I cannot tell
> What power is at work, drenched there
> With purpose, knowing nothing.
>
> (*CP*: 117)

The image in the above lines conveys "the darkness in which we all live, 'knowing nothing'. The earth darkened by rain symbolizes the nightmare blackness that surrounds the modern consciousness" (Cox and Dyson 1963: 150). The main interest of the poem lies in the syllabic metre which Gunn uses. He had earlier admitted that "syllabics were really only a way of teaching myself to write free verse" (Letter 7 Oct. 1972, quoted in Bold 1976: 27). Gunn uses seven syllabics to a line with the rhyme-scheme being ab c abc.

My Sad Captains heralded the emergence of a polished and mature writer for whom strength was now became synonymous with sensibility and endurance. He realized that a strong man was one who had the ability to exist in the world even as a weakling. This poetry attitude continued even in his next volume of poems, *Touch* (1967). The title is indicative of all points of contact—spiritual, physical, emotional—which are endowed with love. The volume contains some of his most profound poems and explores how contrasts can be made with Nature and other human beings. Gunn comments that these poems are "experiences modified by ideas, those ideas in turn are modified by experience and so on endlessly" (Dyson 1990: 17).

"Misanthropos", the longest and most brilliant poem of this collection, is divided into seventeen sections, each having its own individual structure. There is no logical progression of thought from one section to the other but the general theme of the poem is Gunn's vision of human civilization and its development in phases and cycles of birth, decadence, dissolution and rebirth. As Alan Bold sums it up: "The final poem makes a general conclusion.... Man came dust and returns to dust. But...the origin of the human species is not the point: the achievement of humanity is" (Bold 1976: 86).

"Confessions of the Life Artist" is a long poem consisting of ten sections and is considered to be "the last of Gunn's self-conscious poems" (Dyson 1990: 25). The basic thought of the poem is that human life as well as creation is governed by a pre-ordained design which ultimately asserts itself and makes things fall into a set pattern and take final shape. The poem begins with a confident assertion of the main protagonist that he can control his life as an artist and choose and discard aspects of it at will. This makes him:

> buoyant with a sense of choice
> circling over a city
> to reject the thousand and
> to select the one.
>
> ("Poems from the 1960s", *CP*: 159)

However, he is filled with a sense of dread at "the morrow pending" because of the changes inherent in it. He realizes that he has to strike a balance between giving way to his passions and renouncing them completely.

To give way to all passions,
I know, is merely whoring.
Yes, but to give way to none
is to be a whore master.
("Poems from the 1960s", *CP*: 159)

The poet believes that one should have a blind acceptance of the inevitability of birth and death. The whole of God's creation follows its individual principle without any justification or excuse and man should realize that he is just a speck in God's scheme of things and whatever control, he might try to exert on his life, he has to yield eventually to the divine design.

"Touch", the title poem, is Gunn's way of achieving an experience at a psychic and cerebral level. It is an abstract poem and contemplates the inner phenomenon of existence stimulated by an outward reality. Regarding the language of the poem, Martin Dodsworth says,

> Here there is nothing fixed...everything flows. The lines are irregular but...one leads to the next. Due to the shortness of the line, the reader...is compelled to read the lines in a groping way, uncertain where the emphasis may fall.... Their continuity is hesitant, the continuity of exploration and discovery. (Dyson 1990: 20)

The achievements of *Touch* have been aptly summed up by Gunn himself in the following observation:

> I think *Touch* shows a kind of development in attitudes from those of my earlier books.... It is meant to be an allegory for the touch of sympathy that should be the aim of human intercourse.... I do not mean that one can simply love everybody because one wants to, but that one can try to avoid all the situations in which love is impossible. (Poetry Book Society Bulletin: 54, 1967)

Moly (1971), Gunn's fifth collection of poems, belongs to the second phase of his poetic career. It is partly autobiographical, having Gunn's personal experimentation with addictive drugs as its main theme. Some poems also deal with the concept of movement in life. *Moly*, says Thom Gunn, "is my favourite book by myself partly because it's the neglected child. I also think that there I extended my range a great deal...the theme of the book as a whole...is of metamorphosis" (Extract from interview by Haffenden: 1980). It is a collection which represents Thom Gunn's years in San Francisco between 1965-69, specially the time when he started taking drugs at the age of thirty-seven. The half-beast, half-human subject of some of the poems highlight the experience and mental state of the drug user. As Gunn confessed, "it is a personal memoir of myself during these years" (*Poetry Book Society Bulletin*, No. 68 London).

"*Moly*", the title poem, has its origin in Homer's "Odyssey" wherein Ulysses' men had been changed into pigs by Circe. In the poem, the speaker is one of these men who awakens to see his metamorphosis and realizes that his eyes remain his 'only human feature' now. To revive his human self, by 'putting the pig within', he starts searching for a mythical drug named Moly. The implication here is that man is always on a lookout for new and thrilling experiences in an ideal world and needs a kind of drug to hold his inner beast within himself. LSD and other such drugs lift him from a normal level of consciousness and enable him to delve into himself and discover his dimensions whether human or animalistic. The human and animal seem to become interchangeable. To struggle out of his bondage of being 'Buried in Swine', he seeks Moly desperately.

> Cool fresh of Magic in each leaf and shoot,
> From milky flower to the black forked root.
> From this flat dungeon I could rise to skin.
> And human title putting pig within.

The poem is a product of the poet's personal experiences and deals with a desire to have a wider vision and broad experience through drugs. This message is eloquently conveyed through the dramatic tone and compact structure of the poem.

"The Colour Machine" is a fascinating poem with a unique subject-matter and treatment. It presents an LSD (Lysergic Acid Diethyl amide) trip and experience from within and is concerned with a transformed vision under hallucinatory drugs. Openness to experience and the need to articulate a new vision is signified by LSD, according to Gunn. The poem begins with a description of the scene where people are gathered in the basement late in the night for an LSD trip. The Colour-Machine represents the drug with all its flashy intensity. Under the influence of the drug, the poet's friend "switches to green and red" while the poet himself feels that he is "riding through a dark-green sea." This is a highly suggestive, evocative and graphic description of the mental and sensual disintegration which accompanies such a drug-experimentation. It is "a state of unending alternation" in which the material (real) becomes transparent (unreal) and vice versa and ultimately both fuse together and become undistinguishable. The poet remembers a friend who surrendered himself so completely to the Colour Machine that:

> ...plants grew into the bridge—
> of his foot, ears drove through him, he entered
> maries for free. And of course, we never saw him
> again.

The poet is extremely fascinated by such an experience and feels that LSD can help him perceive intense sensory truths. However, his fear of losing the normal and real world keeps him in check. His caution makes him feel "cowardly, selfish and calculating" but simultaneously he wonders "whether he might not have sacrificed some ultimate richness of meaning that is to be found only in the complete surrender of self" (King 1979: 100). In the last few lines, the poet sounds a note of caution against such experiences. He says that even though in our drug-induced state, we consider our mental disintegration "something of negligible importance", yet it would be a real tragedy because our search for psychic significance and thrill is just an illusion. As he puts it in the concluding line, "I am visible and do not know", the poem is not just a superficial account of a drug experience but deals with man's innate desire to move out of his own self and project himself into a world far removed from reality. The poem is divided into two sections or verse paragraphs written in free verse and in a spontaneously eloquent and lucid style.

Most of the poems in *Moly* are written on drug intake and the visions attained by a drug user. All minute observations ranging from its effect on self (*Moly*); on friends (*The Colour Machine*); on strangers (*The Sandman*) and hallucinations (*Tom Dobbin, The Fair in the Woods, The Garden of Gods*) have been given wonderful effects. Gunn's wit, intelligence and superb craftsmanship embodied in the poem leave the readers with the impression of having visited a world of drugs with a master artist.

Jack Straws Castle came after *Moly* and has some echoes of it but the hallucinations and visions of the previous volume are absent here as "Gunn moves into a habit of imaginative participation in the real world as a way of experience" according to Terry Whaler (Whaler 1990: 129). This volume has a number of themes ranging from pre-occupation with California drug culture to the turmoil of mental subjectivity but the central theme is man's realization of his own identity in relation to the reality around.

The collection begins with "*The Bed*", a short poem of two stanzas, which echoes the central theme of the volume, namely man's basic need of establishing his identity. It shows a man and woman lying close to each other in a snow-bound garden. The poem begins with a detailed description of their surroundings wherein boughs are "weighed down" and dead leaves "quilt" the ground. The poet also emphasizes the silent mental communication of the couple who "lie soft-caught" and "loose-twined", "like wrestling statues." Readers are left with an impression of their tenuous physical bonding and the silent internal struggle between them for establishing their separate identities. Thus, Nature becomes an important setting of human drama and its experiences. It is a simple lyrical poem and highlights Gunn's improved command over metrics and integrated imagery.

"Yoko" is considered amongst the best poems not only of this collection but of the entire range of Thom Gunn's poetry. Its uniqueness lies in the fact that the speaker who is also the main subject of the poem is a colossal Newfoundland dog named Yoko. His thoughts, feelings and relationship with his master (who remains silent throughout the poem) is expressed in the most simple and spontaneous language. As Gunn himself says, "I wanted to write a poem that is completely doggy, since so many poems about animals—by Lawrence, Marianne Moore or Ted Hughes—are marvellous, but the subjects are dealt with from a human point of view" (Dyson 1990: 18).

Throughout the day, Yoko sulks in the bottom of a wardrobe, occasionally lumbering across rooms to lap up toilet bowls. His chief happiness is derived from his total love and dedication towards his master "my leader, my love" whose approach delights him:

> What a good man he is,
> I love it when he has the sweat of work on him,
> as he enters I yodel with happiness,...

Going for an evening walk with his master is Yoko's greatest pleasure as he plunges "into the combination of old and new smells"; investigating garbage and the filth around; pissing everywhere. He can also smell the rain in the wind. Such realistic description and the consistent flowing stream of the dog's thoughts and feelings is what make the poem remarkable. The poem ends with an acknowledgement of Yoko's complete self-possession and pride: "My body in its excellent black coat can never let me down." The poem stands in a class by itself. The ingenious imagery and sincerity of feelings attributed to the dog is touching indeed. Though the stanzas are of varying length and structure, they convey a unified thought and testify to Gunn's amazing gift of making any subject worthy of being treated poetically.

"*Jack Straws Castle*" is the last poem of this collection and consists of eleven poems of varying length and structure, the link between them being the main protagonist Jack Straw. The poem uses cerebral images; a dream-reality atmosphere and a psychological slant to achieve a metaphysical probing of self. The theme is individuality and self-consciousness which is inherent in man's basic need to understand himself in the context of external reality. Colin Falck comments that "Jack Straws Castle" "shows a protagonist trapped within one empty castle of the self and trying to decide whether the outside world...is real or only a dream" (quoted in Dyson 1990: 43).

The Passages of Joy (1982) was the next volume of Thom Gunn's poetic output. The title has been taken from Johnson's *Vanity of Human Wishes* and is represented on the cover by a crudely drawn maze. The implication is that 'passages of joy' do not have a centre. All of them narrow and close towards the same, looming darkness. This volume contains many poems which bring out his un-Christian, modern leanings and highlight his philosophy of man moving in dizzying spirals of space and time, a world without end. In such a world, there is nothing like birth and God is either hiding or dead.

Death as a personal loss becomes the theme of the greatest poem in this collection, "A Waking Dream". It was written at the death of Gunn's friend Tony White and despite the undertone of loss that pervades it, Gunn refuses to mourn his friend or treat his death from a moralistic point of view. As we read through the poem, we notice the extensive use of imagery to convey impressions of life and death. Especially noteworthy is the image of the adult game of hide and seek. Gunn sees Tony moving unbowed and calm through the crowd.

> not in the front pushing but not laggard
>
> on his way to the grey river.

The poet tries to catch Tony's eye and even calls out to him but:

> he looks through me and beyond me...
>
> he cannot see who spoke.

The sense of eerieness is further increased as Gunn introduces the theme of nihilism or nothingness as he talks of the 'last camp of experience' where Tony now resides. The metaphysical idea of self-realization and self-exploration in the face of uncompromising external realities is also established. This poem of bereavement consists of seventeen short, lightly-punctuated lines written in free verse.

A fear of bereavement forms an important theme of this collection. No matter how hard Gunn tries to hold on to his reckless and subtle tones in order to alleviate himself from emotions of pain of loss, he cannot help being disturbed when people he loves pass away. This fear of bereavement is adapted to the game of hide and seek which, as Dyson says, keeps "cropping up everywhere: literally child's play to which adults adapt in many odd, off-beat ways. The images are closely linked with labyrinths and may dawn on us gradually" (Dyson 1990: 1176).

Ten years lapsed between the publication of *Passages of Joy* and *The Man with Night Sweats* (1992). This interval is in part attributable to the adjustment (personal and poetic) to watching a generation liquidated by AIDS. Gunn enjoyed a renaissance, following his publication of *The Man with Night Sweats*, a collection which memorialized friends and acquaintances who had fallen victim to AIDS. As Neil Powell, a long-standing but not uncritical admirer puts it:

> In [the final section of the book] Gunn restores poetry to a centrality it has often seemed close to losing, by dealing in the context of a specific human catastrophe with the great themes of life and death, coherently, intelligently, memorably. One could hardly ask for more. (htpp://www.interviews-with-poets.com/thom-gunn/gunn-note.html)

This collection was greeted with great critical acclaim and showed Gunn's increased maturity in terms of the presentation of his subjects. The poems feature real-life situations and everyday problems of the common man. The earlier poems of this collection are a continuation of the theme of *The Passages of Joy*, with reflections on the pleasures and hedonism of homosexual love. However, the concluding section of this volume consists of a sequence of elegies to the poet's friends who had died of AIDS. In fact, some of the finest gay elegies ever written were contained in his collection *The Man with Night Sweats*. These poems are characterised by the contemplation of AIDS sufferers, the bodies that they thought they knew. Yet the greatness of these poems, as works of art, contradicts their ostensible theme of loss.

With the onslaught of AIDS in the 1980s, Gunn, who happened to be a gay poet living in San Francisco at that time, responded with a moving and poignant catalogue of the dead and the dying chronicled in such poems as "To a Dead Graduate Student", "In Time of Plague", "To the Dead Owner of a Gym" and "A Man with Night Sweats". The topicality of the subject earned Gunn the well-deserved comment: "Mr. Gunn is obviously aiming at work on a larger moral scale than most of his contemporaries" (TLS, 3 October 1992). The plague and its increasing casualties was a shattering experience for a sensitive person like Gunn whose pain and helplessness at losing so many of his friends to this epidemic imbued the poems of this volume with a raw vigour and beauty.

"To the Dead Graduate Student" is one of the series of elegies in this volume. The poet expresses his grief and shock at the untimely death of a young graduate student which stunted the possibility of his further growth. The student had wonderful potential and could have been a great and inspiring teacher but nothing had come to fruition because of his death. Gunn uses the apt metaphor of a delicate tendril twining around a hard stalk for growth to describe the possibilities of success which had been wasted.

> The whole rich process of twined opposites,
> Tendril round stalk, developing in tandem
> ...to a unique promise.
>
> (*CP*: 482)

It is a beautifully constructed poem written in simple language and direct style. The pensive and melancholic tone which pervades the poem adds to the sense of pathos of the situation described.

A perusal of the poems reveals the long journey which Gunn had made in his craft. From a young and headstrong rebel, he had blossomed into a mature poet with immense potential. He had reached a point where his contact with his readers was direct and immediate because of his intelligible language and absence of myths or allusions to drive home a point. *The Man with Night Sweats* thus reinstated him as a great poet who well deserved the critical acclaim which its publication brought him.

It took another eight years before Gunn's twelfth and last volume of poems, *Boss Cupid*, was published in 2000. It shows the seventy-one-year old Gunn in a retrospective and surprisingly revealing mood. Details of his personal life which he had hitherto been circumspect about, or just hinted at obliquely, find vivid expressions in the poems of this volume. Critics opine that his confessional mood was brought on by his overpowering need to relive his childhood and youth in the twilight of his life. The cover page describes it as a book containing, "poems by the quintessential San Francisco poet, who is a quintessential craftsman and a quintessential love poet, though not of quintessential love" (Gunn: 2000). Earlier Gunn had displayed a definite aversion to writing poems featuring love and trust between human beings, but in *Boss Cupid*, named after Cupid, the God of love, Gunn has expressed himself in the mellowest of words about trust being the base of any human relationship. Thus, we find Gunn becoming much more expansive, mature and tolerant in his later verse, thereby making these poems "a startling and eloquent gloss on wanton want, moving freely from the story of a king David and Bathsheba to Arthur Rimbaud's diet to the taste of Jeffery Dahmer" (Gunn, *Boss Cupid*, Cover page: 2000).

The poems in *Boss Cupid* are a mixed bag and it is impossible to determine a single, dominant theme in this collection. The volume has a sobering start and opens with a moving elegy to Gunn's friend, Robert Duncan, in the poem "Duncan". This is followed by two poems on his mother's suicide—"My Mother's Pride" and "The Gas Poker". There are psychological poems on despair and fatalism (e.g. "A Young Novelist"), historical ones revealing his scepticism of art and religion (e.g. "The Antagonism"), poems on sex (e.g. "Iron Man" and "Coffee Shop"), daringly imaginative songs on the serial killer Jeffery Dahmer and finally mellowed, recuperative poems on faith, love and trust like those on King David. Yet, through it all, we have Thom Gunn exploring his 'self' in these poems.

The sombre tones of the poems on death and lament which feature in the first section of *Boss Cupid* undergo a change in its second section. The tension eases as Gunn adopts a more relaxed and open attitude. "Office Hours", which is a candid appraisal of the poet's professional life as an English Professor, is one such poem. This is the first time that he confesses how much he enjoyed teaching and interacting with his students.

These big handsome
Sweaty boys,
these sharp chic
ironic girls
with brisk hairstyles
and subtle tattoos
(*Boss Cupid*: 77-78)

His rapport with his students, the closeness and sense of friendship that he experiences with them compensates for any drawback which he might have faced in his career.

Gunn stresses that his relationship with his students is thoroughly professional, impersonal and free from any hint of sexuality. His students and he "do not flirt with another" but together they flirt with the poet who is part of their curriculum. The poem has an informal tone and a relaxed style. Interestingly, the entire poem does not have any punctuation marks. It begins with the small letter 't' and continues in short sentences till the end. A vivid picture of the teaching profession is thus created.

The final poem of the collection, "In Trust" is suggestive of the poet's journey: from fragmentation to wholeness, from disbelief and cynicism to trust and love. Gunn never felt apologetic about being a homosexual and was critical of the bondage, possessiveness and jealousy which formed an inevitable part of heterosexual relationship. More than sexuality, what he cherished was a sense of affinity and brotherhood that he shared with his partner wherein each gave the other his private space and independence in mutual trust. Gunn knew that they might get separated from one another for long periods, go out with different boyfriends but at the end of it all, they would come back to each other.

As you began
You'll end the year with me.

We'll hug each other while we can,
Work or stray while we must.
Nothing is or will ever be,
Mine, I suppose. No one can hold a heart,
But what we hold in trust
We do hold, even apart.
(*Boss Cupid*: 96-97)

Gunn here displays his courage of conviction and firm faith in trust and understanding being the binding factor between two people in love with each other. The language is simple and the treatment of an obviously unconventional theme is characteristically direct. Gunn once again displays his technical virtuosity in the metrics, structure, imagery and tonal quality of the poem.

Thus concluded, with *Boss Cupid*, the third and final phase of Thom Gunn's poetic career. Reading his poetry, one cannot help marvelling at the extraordinary range of his subjects and his depth of observation and sensitivity while handling his varying themes. His themes range from the torments of middle-class life in the post-war scenario to a celebration of life, made possible, through chemically-induced spirituality. He cynically writes about the human and animal instincts coexisting in man, with the same ease that he displays while describing the mesmerizing effect of Nature in an awed tone. Poems about sex and drugs are written alongside those on love and trust. He has been called a poet of violence by various critics but his contemporary and competitor, Ted Hughes, describes him as the gentlest of human beings. His elegies on the death of his friends and acquaintances, during the AIDS epidemic, have immortalized him as a poet. In all his moods, attitudes and perceptions, he comes across as a consummate artist and readers echo the sentiments expressed in his poem "Tamer and the Hawk":

You sealed me with your love
The habit of your words
Has hooded me....

Poetry must be magnificently achieved, or it is negligible but very few writers manage to sustain the special verbal and emotional intensity that poetry requires across their whole career. However Thom Gunn, appearing in the fifties, kept writing in top form for five decades, till he died at the age of seventy-four in 2004. His particular genius has been to embody the human and artistic contradictions of his age not only as a poet but also as a perceptive critic of gay poetry. As a major Gay poet, Gunn's influence can be seen on such other gay poets as Edgar Bowers, Michael Vince, Jim Powell, Robert Wells and Gregory Woods. One of the most exciting and challenging bodies of poetry created over the past 50 years, Gunn's *Collected Poems* (1994) offers a heady Anglo-American cocktail of liberal sensuality often contained within surprisingly conventional forms. His poetry is the account of an existential quest, a pursuit of a sense of personal identity and meaning in a world where the traditional supports for life's meaning are being questioned.

Even at seventy-four (when he passed away), with his urbane involvement and celebration of life and his associations with counter-culture, one never thought of him as ageing. He will be remembered as a transatlantic poet and critic, a hugely respected figure in twentieth-century poetry and a liberal moralist.

WORKS CITED

A.E. Dyson. *Three Contemporary Poets*. London: Macmillan, 1990.

Alvarez, A. *The New Poetry*. Hardmondworth: Penguin, 1962.

Bold, Alan. *Thom Gunn and Ted Hughes*. Edinburgh: Oliver and Boyd, 1976.

Conquest, Robert. (ed.) *New Lines*. London: Macmillan, 1967.

Enright, D.J. Poets of the 1950's. Tokyo: 17 Kenkyusha Press. 1955.

John, Haffenden. "Experience and Ideas: An Interview with Thom Gunn". Craig Raine and Richard Boston. (ed.) *Quarto*, July 1980.

Gunn, Thom. *Boss Cupid*. U.S.A.: Farrar, Strawe and Giroux, 2000.

Gunn, Thom. The Sense of Movement. London: Faber and Faber, 1968.

Morrison, Blake. *The Movement*. Great Britain: New OUP, 1980.

Perkins, David. *A History of Modern Poetry: Modernism and After.* Cambridge: Harvard UP, 1976.

Ramanan, Mohan. *The Movement.* Delhi: B.R. Publications, 1989.

Schmidt. M. (ed.) *Eleven British Poets.* London: Mutheun and Co. Ltd., 1980.

Scott, F.D. "In the Movement". *The Spectator.* 1st Oct., 1954.

Sturney, Michael L. *Critical Survey of Poetry.* New Jersey: Salem Press, 1982.

Thwaite, Anthony. *Poetry Today: A Critical Guide to British Poetry.* London and NY: Longmans, 1985.

Wilmer, Clive. "My Life Upto Now." *The Occasions of Poetry.* London: Faber, 1982.